T0266450

ALIVE

HIJACKED BY THE HOLY SPIRIT

CHARLOTTE BENKE

Carpenter's Son Publishing

Published by Carpenter's Son Publishing, Franklin, Tennessee

Published in association with Larry Carpenter of Christian Book Services, LLC
www.christianbookservices.com

Edited by Nonie Jobe

Cover and Interior Design by Adept Content Solutions

Printed in the United States of America

978-1-942587-92-7

CONTENTS

FOREWORD
BY NONIE JOBE

CHARLOTTE AND I MET by divine appointment at a Christian writers' conference. I had spent the morning struggling to hear, with the bad acoustics on my side of the room in tandem with my hearing challenges. Sometime after lunch, I moved to the middle of the room so I could hear better; I ended up at Charlotte's table. Prior to my moving, the emcee had given me a great plug as a "go-to" editor as I went forward to collect a door prize.

Charlotte told me later she had prayed for three things before she came to the conference: a publisher, an editor, and a friend. Larry Carpenter, the publisher of this book, was there that day, and Charlotte met with him after the conference. I filled the other two slots. Charlotte and I have become friends through the process of getting her book ready for publishing. Due to various challenges in our personal lives, our friendship motto has become: *I'll pray for you and you pray for me!*

Charlotte told me that day that she thought her book may be too long, at about 205,000 words. Gulp! I encouraged her to shorten it to about 75,000 words, and I would look at the manuscript at that point to see if we needed to reduce it even more. We had an initial meeting while she was still in the reduction process, and I got really excited about the book's concept. Months went by as she reduced the size of the book, and we corresponded by email many times. When she was ready to turn it over to me, we actually met in my husband's hospital room for the thumb drive handover and contract signing. That was Charlotte's idea; she wanted us to meet there so she could pray for my husband and me. I knew from just meeting with her for the second time and emailing back and forth that she had a special "sold-out" relationship with God. Though I'm her senior by several decades, I told God, "I want to be like her when I grow up!"

I have to say that I was not prepared for what I found in the book. First, Charlotte is "refreshingly blunt" in her journal entries, and I was surprised that she was willing and brave enough to share many of them. I realized, though, that those entries—frank and revealing as they were—would serve a purpose, as many of her readers would heavily relate to where she was at that stage in her life.

Second, the early Charlotte was nothing like the Charlotte I had come to know, and it was hard for me to imagine her any other way. If I did not know the life-altering power of God, I would never have believed the transformation that took place from the old Charlotte to the new—it was clearly a "night versus day" transformation. The old Charlotte was insecure, unloving, and shallow, and her happiness depended solely upon the status of her relationships. When she became a Christian, she began to change, but it was not as instantaneous as many people believe it will be. God changes line upon line and precept upon precept. We *wish* He would do surgery on us and change us instantly; but that kind of change is neither lasting nor deep, nor does it prepare us to serve Him well. Often His "surgery" of choice is to use life circumstances and, yes, people and pain, over a period of time, to mold us into His image. God's people are always a "work in progress."

One of the hardest things Charlotte had to learn was that her source of happiness was God and no one else. That was a part of the book that I really got excited about, because I've known so many people over my lifetime who have struggled with that. I have known many single women, especially, who believed, "If I could only find a husband, my life would be better." I have known childless women who believed, "If I could only conceive and bear a child, my life would be complete." I have also known men who believed, "If I could get out of this marriage and find a different wife, I would be happy." If you find yourself trapped in that kind of thinking, I pray that this book will expose those wrong beliefs, and you will discover, as Charlotte did, that earthly relationships will *never* fill the huge hole in your heart. And neither will earthly possessions or achievements.

By the time you get to the end of the book, you will be as amazed as I was at the transformed Charlotte. But more than that, your heart will be overjoyed at the mercy, patience, and transforming power of God! Charlotte's life is a living testament to His love, grace, and might, and that is her whole purpose for writing this book. Only God could have changed her into a new person with new priorities and a new purpose. Only God could have filled her heart with peace, joy, love, and contentment despite her pain and struggles. God, and *only* God can do the same for you!

PREFACE

Lyrics by MercyMe

"The Hurt and the Healer"

Breathe
Sometimes I feel it's all that I can do
Pain so deep that I can hardly move
Just keep my eyes completely fixed on you
Lord, take hold and pull me through

So here I am
What's left of me
Where glory meets my suffering

I'm alive
Even though a part of me has died
You take my heart and breathe it back to life
I'll fall into your arms open wide
When the hurt and the healer collide[1]

INTRODUCTION

WELCOME ABOARD the ALIVE aircraft! You are about to embark on my personal journey of surrender and self-discovery. All are invited—males and females, married and unmarried, Christians and non-Christians—because regardless of who you are, this book was written for *you*. I pray that you will be deeply impacted and walk away changed. Until then, sit back, relax, and enjoy the flight!

A Message from the Cockpit:

I started writing this book in January 2016, after much anticipation and prayer. It was my second week of unemployment, and I knew that I was embarking on a special assignment. I did not know how the process would unfold or how long it would take, but I *knew* that God had given me an overwhelming desire to write my testimony and to share it with others.

God has done so much in my life that I could not fit it all within these pages! Even my journals don't contain all the stories, adventures, trials, and heartache that I have experienced. They do offer snapshots —moments in time—of my life over the years. These moments range from amazing to less-than-flattering, and I share them with you openly, to paint a vivid picture of my past and to show you how I have changed through developing a personal relationship with Jesus Christ.

My journals are precious recordings of my life—pieces of me captured on paper. As I reviewed them in preparation for writing this book, I realized that my past was heavily marked with the fingerprints of God. Even before I started seeking Him, God was there behind the scenes, in control of everything, including my life. Since accepting Jesus as my Lord and Savior in my twenties, my life has a deeper meaning and purpose. He has changed me into a new person and given me new desires. The Bible refers to this as being "born again" (John 3:3, John 3:7, and 1 Peter 1:23) and "transformed by the renewing of the mind" (Romans 12:2). It is a complex and gradual process that occurs over time, but it does not happen automatically.

At times I have struggled to accept God's plan for my life, both as a young convert and as a committed follower. Letting go of the desires of your heart is difficult, especially when you are surrounded by people who seemingly have what you want: a fulfilling career, a loving spouse, a close-knit family, and deeply connected friendships. These are all good desires, but they cannot take the place of our *ultimate* desire, the reason we were created—to love God, to know God, and to serve Him by loving others.

I have learned much and grown much as a follower of Jesus. The purpose of my life is to share my testimony of faith and transformation in Christ with as many people as possible. I desire to glorify God and to encourage others to live for Him with their whole hearts. My story is *about* God and I am writing it *for* God. May His name be praised forever and ever! Amen.

NOTES BEFORE TAKEOFF

- Occasionally in PART I, I inject the thoughts I had while I was going through a particular experience; those thoughts are in present tense and *italic* font.

- I decided to write all 3s and 7s as numerals for two reasons. First, they are special numbers to God throughout the Bible. The number 3 signifies the Trinity (God the Father, God the Son, and God the Holy Spirit). The number 7 indicates perfection, fulfillment, and completion. Secondly, I noticed many occurrences of 3s and 7s throughout my journal entries, and I wanted to draw your attention to them.

- Many of the names in this book have been changed out of respect and privacy for the individual. I have not included personal stories to embarrass anyone; my desire is simply to show where I was at each stage of my life and how God used a variety of different people and hardships to shape me closer into His image.

- In PART II, text from my journals is indented. These partial entries show my inner transformation over time. They have been edited for spelling, grammar, word count, and readability. Key themes, wisdom, foreshadowing, and select references to God are in **bold**.

- Journal entry titles, clarifications, and modifications are in square brackets [ ].

- Parentheses ( ) are part of my original journal entry.

Part I

The Aerial View

CHAPTER 1

MY FLIGHT CREW

GOD PLACES US IN FAMILIES, and He uses those families and our environment to shape us. When we finally allow it, He uses all of the qualities we inherit from our parents, along with our wounds, scars, and brokenness, to transform us into a new creation that more closely resembles Him and His loving nature.

When I entered the world through my mother's womb, 3 of my four grandparents were deceased. My only living grandparent was my mom's mother, Emma. When my mother was only thirteen years old, her father drove home drunk from the bar one night. He hit a truck on the side of the road and died instantly. Although she loved Jesus, my grandmother never overcame the grief of losing her husband—she had put her hope and security in him.

My mother's brother never recovered from the tragedy either. He wanted a new life, so he enlisted in the army against my grandmother's wishes. He numbed his pain with alcohol and cigarettes and died from cancer when I was in college. I didn't know my Uncle Jerry, but I remember visiting his farm as a young girl and playing on the rope swing inside the barn. My only memory of him is his sitting in a lawn chair wearing a white T-shirt and jeans, smoking and laughing. My mother told me he had a habit of using bad language, and he was angry at God.

My grandmother Emma passed away when I was twenty-one. I remember playing cards and eating ice cream with her as a child, but we really didn't interact much. She didn't drive, nor did she maintain friendships, so her life was very lonely. Mom said she cried herself to sleep for many years. My only living grandparent was unable to give and receive affection. Consequently, she was emotionally distant and I did not feel loved by her.

My mother was the sole survivor from her family. She overcame her father's death and continued to live a fruitful life. Raised in the Lutheran church and a believer in Jesus Christ, she accepted God's will and her father's death as a young teenager. She matured into a humble, loyal, and gracious lady.

As I was growing up, my mother resembled June Cleaver, the iconic television character from *Leave it to Beaver*. Her hair and clothes were always neat and tidy, her manners well-polished. She spent hours in the kitchen preparing the family meals. Everything she did, she did with love.

My mother has always valued appearance and cleanliness. She kept up the household well during all those years. When she was finished inside, she would work in the yard raking leaves, sweeping walkways, and planting flowers. She rarely sat down to enjoy the work of her hands, and there was little time to read, watch television, or maintain friendships. She was completely devoted to serving and nurturing her family.

My father, born and raised in Germany before World War II, was drafted into the German army at the age of seventeen. He was an excellent sharpshooter who received several metals for bravery and marksmanship. One day near the end of the war, he took cover in a foxhole and an American tank passed overhead. The crumbling dirt around him severely crushed his left leg. The military doctor wanted to amputate to prevent gangrene; but my father was not a man to surrender, and he refused to consent. He was later discharged and worked very hard to recover the use of his leg with only a slight limp.

In his twenties, my father moved to America and taught himself English by watching movies. He lived as a bachelor and had many friends from different countries. (His roommate Jim would later become the father of my childhood friend, Renee. Her name appears throughout my story.) Less than two decades later, my father met my mother at a Volkswagen dealership in Michigan, and they married after a short courtship.

My father is a man of extraordinary talents. He is frugal, hardworking, and disciplined—a planner, with a sharp mind and excellent memory. Though he has an abundance of admirable qualities, he lacked the ability to give verbal and physical affection during my childhood. I do not recall receiving many hugs, smiles, or words of encouragement from him. His critical mind and quick temper suppressed my developing self-confidence. Perfection seemed to be his standard, and I tried my best to measure up. (I'm pleased to say that he's now more affectionate, thanks to his grandkids and the power of prayer!)

My brother, who is 3 years older, is my only sibling. He is kind, hardworking, and highly intelligent, with a doctorate degree in Nuclear Engineering. He married his college sweetheart, who is as driven and career-focused as he is. They have two beautiful daughters and live in the great state of Texas.

That's an overview of my family: an emotionally distant grandmother, a nurturing mother, a stern father, and a genius brother. I have aunts, uncles, and cousins, but they are all distant. Because my father's relatives are in Europe and my mother has kept herself distanced from hers, I have not known my extended family. Ultimately, God used the emotional and physical distance to shape the independent woman I have become.

Chapter 2

Solo Passenger

MY NAME IS CHARLOTTE Joanna Marianne Benke. I was named after my Grandmother Charlotte, my father's mother, who died in Germany before I was born. My two middle names are a tribute to my mother and my father's twin sister.

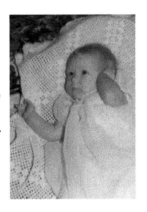

I grew up in Troy, Michigan, with a dear friend Renee, who lived down the street. She has known and loved me since I was 3 years old. (Renee had prayed for my salvation long before I realized I needed a Savior, and she has witnessed my transformation in Christ.) My family did not attend church, not even on Christmas or Easter. But even though I didn't know about God's unconditional love for me during those years, I believed He existed.

When I was 3 years old, I got glasses—bifocals—to correct a lazy eye. In those days, bifocals were thick and unattractive, and they drew negative attention. Some kids asked why I had a line in the center of my glasses. Others said their grandma had glasses like mine. I wore bifocals until I was fifteen, so I spent twelve years of my life "being different."

The older I grew, the more self-conscious I became about my glasses. When I wore them, my eyes looked larger because of the magnification. When I took them off, my right eye turned inward toward my nose. Curious kids asked, "What's wrong with your eye?" It made sleepovers and pool parties a bit awkward, and I did not enjoy the extra attention.

In middle school, I played the clarinet and earned the coveted rank of First Chair. Originally, I had wanted to play the flute like the other girls, but my brother persuaded me to play the clarinet. "I mean, look!" he said. "We already have one in the basement!" (I think my parents put him up to the task.) Despite my talent and sense of accomplishment, I didn't continue playing the clarinet in high school for fear of being labeled a "band geek." I just wanted to fit in.

The summer before ninth grade I did something I'd never done before: I tried out for a school sport. I chose tennis because it was a nice individual sport, and I had taken some lessons over the summer. Basketball, volleyball, and soccer required aggression and stamina, and I had neither. I was timid and shy, tall and awkward. When the coach cut me before the last day of tryouts, it was just one more validation of my self-worth: *I'm not good enough.* Playing on the tennis team had been my glimmer of hope for peer acceptance.

Shortly after, a friend suggested we try out for the high school dance/drill team, "just for fun." *Ha, ha, right! I've had less than a year of dance lessons.* But I gave in and faced my fears of experiencing another public rejection. The dance routines and practices were intense. I couldn't do the splits or high kicks, but each night I practiced at home, over and over, until I mastered the moves. I was a slow learner; but by repetition, I programmed my mind and body to perform the routines. On the last day of tryouts, we performed for the coaches. To my shock, none of my friends— the ones with years of dance experience—were selected. *There's no way I'm going to make it! But wait! Was that my name that was called?* I was finally accepted for something I wouldn't be teased about! Who knew the former band geek with braces and bifocals could dance?

Making the drill team was an unexpected dream come true. But even better was the day I was fitted for contact lenses at the start of my sophomore year. No more bifocals! No more standing out! No more teasing! My self-esteem increased, but I still felt far from beautiful. I did not like myself on the inside.

I graduated with honors from Troy High School in 1994. My brother and my chemistry teacher both encouraged me to study Chemical Engineering in college, so I did. Apparently "Chem E" was the most challenging undergraduate degree at the University of Michigan, and it nearly killed me! Grouped with some of the brightest minds from across the country, I stressed out striving for As and Bs. My self-esteem took another blow. Studies took precedence over family and friends, and my self-worth became proportional to my performance. When I received a 42 percent on a heat and mass transfer exam, I felt like a failure. Even with a class curve of twenty-five points, making my grade a 67 percent, it was unacceptable. *I must work harder and study longer!*

My self-imposed pressure created overwhelming anxiety, cystic acne, and weight gain. Although I went to a Big Ten university, I only attended one football game during my entire four years there. My weekends were consumed at the library inside a small cubical with a desk, chair, door, and a window to the outside world. Fun was only scheduled in if there was time.

My college years were the most intense of my life. I cringe when I recall the type of person I was—stressed out and so very selfish. God, in His grace (although I didn't recognize it at the time), gave me Steff and Lisa as study buddies. Our theme song our senior year was  Gloria Gaynor's "I Will Survive." Without the support of these two friends, I'm sure I wouldn't have. In May 1998, the 3 of us proudly graduated with honors.

Prior to graduation, I signed up for two campus interviews— one for technical sales and one for engineering—with the Lincoln Electric Company, a worldwide manufacturer of welding equipment and consumables. I barely knew what welding was and did not desire to pursue a sales career. At the end of the first interview, the recruiter said, "I see you're on the schedule to come back tomorrow.

That won't be necessary. Tell me which pile to put your resume in—the one for sales or engineering?" I opened my mouth to say "engineering," but what came out was "sales." The recruiter replied, "Thank you for your time. I'll be in touch." I walked out dazed and confused. *What just happened? Me, in sales?* Quiet, shy, and insecure, I was definitely not the typical salesperson.

A few weeks later, as I toured Lincoln Electric's headquarters in Ohio, I had a strong gut feeling that I should take the job if they made me an offer. Even though the position was in sales and welding, two areas I knew nothing about, the feeling was strong. The following week, I received a written offer and accepted it with excitement. The job required that I relocate twice—once to Cleveland for training and again to wherever my sales territory was, somewhere in the United States.

 I met Amy after I moved to Cleveland in June 1998. Since the welding industry is male-dominated, we were the only two females in a training class of eighteen. I was uncomfortable, but Amy fit in immediately. She was a welding engineer, a Daddy's girl, and engaged to be married, and she loved football, beer, and attention from guys. She was everything I wasn't.

During the first 3 months of training, we learned to weld in a non-air-conditioned manufacturing plant. At "weld school," we each wore a long-sleeved polyester Lincoln shirt, jeans, leathers, a welding helmet, gloves, and steel-toed boots. Pause and picture it: Charlotte, the timid but feminine city girl who grew up with Barbies and bifocals, was welding with a bunch of dudes!

Welding was sweaty, dirty, and dangerous. Some days I cried in the locker room out of sheer frustration. Learning to weld was challenging, and I practiced all day with few breaks. I was determined to learn; and just as I did when I was part of the dance/drill team, I repeated the steps relentlessly until I learned the technique. One special day, I was recognized for having the best flux-cored vertical-up weld in the class—better than the welding engineer from Texas A&M University! Everyone was amazed, including myself.

With continued determination, I completed the technical sales training program in early 1999. I was placed on a special assignment in Indiana assisting a large robotic welding customer. I worked as the onsite Lincoln representative for twelve hours  a day, 7 days a week, with every other weekend off. My eyes got so dry and tired that I took a break from wearing either my contact lenses or my backup pair of glasses.

Then a funny thing happened. Days without my glasses or contacts turned into weeks, and weeks turned into months. One day I suddenly realized that I no longer needed corrective lenses. My lazy eye was gone and my vision was fine! God had healed my eyes!

Is there any other explanation?

CHAPTER 3

TURBULENCE AND
LOSS OF CABIN PRESSURE

IN THE SUMMER OF 1999, I relocated to Texas to begin my sales career. Marie lived in the apartment below mine, and she became my only Texas friend. We hung out at trendy restaurants, bars and clubs, where we danced and met guys. I was drawn into the Dallas lifestyle of wealth, beauty, and social drinking.

In the spring of 2000, I bought my first new car. All the cars in my family had been previously owned up to this point. My father was frugal and had saved enough money to pay for my college education. I had learned well from him and also saved money from each paycheck. When the air conditioning went out in my used Mercury Sable, I went car shopping.

My new Nissan Maxima (aka "Maximus") was beautiful. It had luxury features and sport performance, and yet it was practical for my welding sales career. I felt like a rock star.
My first new car! I also felt guilty because it was much nicer than anything I had owned. *Maybe it's too nice, too flashy?*

My personal insecurities continued as I settled into Texas. I became a workaholic, like a prisoner chained to a nonstop sales treadmill. There was always more to achieve, new products to learn, monthly contests to win, and training programs to conduct, as well as product promotions, open houses, cold calls, and territory sales goals. There was no finish line—ever. Customers didn't stay satisfied and problems arose frequently. I struggled to juggle the continuous needs of my customers, distributors, coworkers, and sales managers.

After years of pouring energy into my career and living for myself on the weekends, I burned out. My life was out of balance, leaving me unfulfilled, discontented, and disillusioned. In January 2002, Marie invited me to church. I had never attended a regular service—only a few weddings and funerals. Several people had tried sharing Christ with me in the past, including Renee, but I refused to listen. My walls were up and my heart was hard. I had no interest in hearing about God or Jesus.

I hesitated to accept Marie's invitation; but since I was desperate for some kind of peace, I eventually agreed to go. Fellowship Church was unlike anything I had seen or imagined. Thousands of people filled up stadium-like seating, and I discovered there were five services every weekend. As I attended week after week, it felt like Pastor Ed was speaking directly to me! The songs made me weep, and yet my heart was far from God.

Exactly 7 days after my first visit to church, I worked a Dallas hardware show with a Lincoln salesman from my training class. When his friend Jake came to our booth, my first thought was, *Wow. He's hot!* Jake had dark hair and piercing eyes. My next thought was, *He's way out of my league.* Late that night, I joined a coworker, Jake, and other vendors in Deep Ellum. After a few drinks, I found out that Jake thought I was gorgeous. I was shocked—no guy *that* good looking was *ever* interested in me!

My attraction to Jake was intense. He made me feel beautiful in a way I had not experienced. He asked me out for dinner the following evening; it was surreal and our night unfolded like a dream. When he returned to Chicago, we remained in touch through emails and phone calls. I was smitten. Jake made me feel alive.

I continued attending Sunday services even when Marie didn't. Slowly my heart softened to God's Word. It was a new and unusual experience, feeling something moving around inside my soul. Each encounter was emotional, and I cried a lot. God was conducting spiritual business that I didn't understand at the time. Shame and guilt bubbled up, but the truth and hope of God's love drew me back week after week. While my mind and heart were slowly changing, I still lived the same, did not own a Bible, and Marie was still my only friend in Dallas.

While Jake and I were drawing closer, though, Marie and I started growing apart. Our friendship silently disintegrated, despite my preservation attempts. I didn't know how to talk to her about the rift, so I did what I learned growing up—I pushed the hurt and resentment deep inside and attempted to move on.

I continued attending church alone, and God continued planting seeds in my heart. Jake returned to Dallas for another show and we reunited. Over a few beers, I excitedly told him about my church, and he told me he was agnostic. My heart sank. *Maybe I can convert him to Christianity. Is that God's plan?*

Jake promised repeatedly to visit me apart from work, and I waited eagerly for him to fulfill that promise. But instead of the flight itinerary I expected in my inbox, I received a lengthy email explaining why he wasn't coming. He told me he had met someone in Chicago, and that a long-distance relationship with me was impractical. He said he deeply admired me and was very sorry. I was devastated! Jake had been my escape from life, from a stressful job, and from reality. I thought I needed him to be happy, to feel loved and accepted. I cried all weekend. *No more Marie and now no more Jake?* It was more than I could bear.

However, I kept going to church.

CHAPTER 4
RESCUE TAKEOVER

ON A FRIDAY NIGHT a few weeks later, I turned on the television. I was still grappling with the pain of being rejected by two people, one right after the other. *Maybe there is something wrong with me?* After a hot bath, I heated a frozen dinner and flipped channels looking for something to watch. I paused on an unknown channel, where a young pastor was speaking. I had previously made fun of TV preachers and joked about people "staying home to read their Bibles." Still wounded from Jake's rejection, though, I was drawn to listen.

At the end of the program, the pastor invited his audience to acknowledge Jesus as the Son of God, who died for them so that their sins could be forgiven. He led us in a prayer that confessed our need for a Savior and asked God to forgive our sins and to take control of our lives. Feeling the weight of my brokenness, I knelt down at my sofa wearing a bathrobe and hair towel. I prayed for Jesus to come into my life and to forgive my sins. When the prayer was over, I got up and ate dinner and went about life as normal. I didn't feel different, nor was I aware of the *significant* impact of what I had just done. I didn't expect anything to change, but little did I know that the Holy Spirit "hijack" was already taking place!

The next month, I met Amanda at a summer painting class. She also attended Fellowship Church and invited me to visit a Bible study. I felt certain I wasn't ready to be in a room full of Christians who were singing and sharing "the love of the Lord," but Amanda persisted. I asked her if they were going to "pray and stuff" at their meetings. She smiled sweetly and said, "I don't think so." Well, she lied. ☺

The group was called a home team, and it was made up of singles in their twenties and thirties. I was the baby believer of the group, and I was nervous, embarrassed, and ignorant. They were very welcoming, and I was surprised at how quickly I made friends—Christian ones. Marie was officially out of my life, but God blessed me with caring people who accepted me as I was.

Through home team and weekly church services, I started learning about Jesus, God, prayer, tithing, serving, and baptism. My heart and mind began changing. I stopped using bad language without even trying; God removed select words from my vocabulary seemingly overnight. Working in the welding industry, I had been exposed to "colorful" language and had started talking like some of the welders. When I was frustrated, the bad words had flowed freely. Well, not anymore!

In addition to a shortened vocabulary, I lost the desire to frequent bars and clubs. Instead, I attended Saturday night services with my home team. I experienced God's peace and joy during stressful work situations. My lonely world of one broadened as I met more people who knew Jesus or needed to meet Jesus. Several customers noticed a difference; one even asked if I was in love! I wasn't dating anyone—the transformation was all because of Jesus Christ.

 In September 2002, a welding customer in Fort Worth bought me my first Bible. In the months prior, I had gone to home team empty handed. I was introduced to Christian radio stations and bookstores, and I began seeing life through a renewed pair of eyes. I started volunteering in the church preschool and began tithing. My heart was on fire for the Lord, and I began inviting people to church. I knew the truth, and it had set me free!

On June 21, 2003, approximately one year after Jake broke my heart, I was baptized. As I stood in the long line, I noticed the

crowd of cheering people. No one from
my family was there, but several home
team friends were. When my name was
called, I walked toward the pool with a
pounding heart. As I entered the water,
peace washed over me and the noise
inside my mind went silent. My body
relaxed. I was baptized by immersion, in
the name of the Father, the Son, and the
Holy Spirit.

(Note: Going under the water represents the death of the old self.
The rising out of the water represents the resurrection of new life
in Christ. The act of baptism didn't save me from my sins; it was
an outward expression of my inward commitment to follow Jesus. I
received eternal salvation the night I prayed with the TV pastor, and
it was then that the Holy Spirit established a dwelling place inside
me.)

With wet hair and soaking clothes, I scurried to the nearest
ladies' room. Of the thousands of people who attended my
megachurch, who should I lock eyes with as I entered the restroom?
Marie! We hadn't spoken in a year. I had wished to never see her
again, but there she was. *Should I look away or say something?*
The Spirit of the Lord was on me, and I held her gaze. I smiled and
walked toward her. In a blur of an exchange, we reconciled. Marie
congratulated me on my baptism and introduced me to her friend
Dianna, who was also baptized that night.

It felt incredible to forgive Marie—the burden was *finally* lifted!
I know without a doubt that God planned that meeting. It was my
first test after baptism, and it was a big one. Thankfully, I passed!
Looking back, I see how the Lord used Marie, Jake, and other trials
and disappointments to bring me to my knees and into His kingdom.
Glory be to God!

CHAPTER 5

FLYING WITH THE HOLY SPIRIT

IN APRIL 2003, I bought my first house. By October, I was hosting home team and serving in the singles ministry with greeters and first-time visitors. Eventually, I transitioned into assisting the leaders with event planning and

coordinating volunteers. I had found my place to serve, and it felt amazing!

During my eight years at Fellowship Church, God matured me; and yet I still had much to learn. By the end of 2009, I found myself in a spiritual wilderness. The services were no longer ministering to me, the singles ministry restructured, and friendships had faded. Attempts to make new friends were unfruitful and discouraging. Week after week, I felt alone and disconnected. My heart was burdened, and I thought something was out of place within me. I prayed about the dryness, asking God for understanding and direction.

After months of prayer, the Lord spoke to me by 3 different means. First, I stumbled across a broadcast from Hillsong Church where Pastor Brian Houston spoke about letting go if God is finished in a certain area. Two days later, on the same station, I flipped on Joyce Meyer's program. She talked about having courage to make changes in order to keep growing in the Word of God. Through both messages, the Holy Spirit nudged me to let go of Fellowship Church.

After the Hillsong broadcast, however, something special happened. I left the room to process the reality of what I just heard.

Perhaps I should attend Fellowship every other weekend so I can still serve in the singles ministry and visit churches on the other Sundays. Suddenly and clearly God spoke into my mind, "When something is dead, should you let go completely or partially?" Instantly my spirit replied, "Completely." I had my answer after months of prayer—I was to let go and move in a new direction. Like Abraham in the Old Testament, I did not know where to go.

Two years earlier, I had met Dong in spin class, who attended Irving Bible Church. I had also heard good things about The Village Church. So in February 2010, I visited both churches looking for my new home. Irving Bible Church had just begun a new series on the 7 deadly sins. Through the music and teachings, God's Spirit moved again in my heart. Conviction and tears followed. My ears were opened, and the dryness was gone!

At the age of thirty-four, I replanted myself at Irving Bible Church. I visited Thrive, the singles class for thirty- and forty-somethings, and was warmly accepted. I became a greeter and hosted numerous events in my home. Two years later, I was invited to serve as the social coordinator, with the responsibility of planning lunches, potlucks, and several social activities a month. I accepted the position after some prayer, knowing it would be a large time commitment. My time, effort, and energy were spent on enhancing our Christian singles fellowship. After several months, a new burden grew in my heart: *Who are we ministering to? Who among us is being healed or transformed?*

Near the end of 2012, the dryness returned. My connection with the singles group faded, and I felt unsettled. Once again, I wondered if there was something out of place within me. *Am I harboring unforgiveness or resentment?* I prayed and waited for an answer, and then I decided to take a break from Thrive, hoping understanding would come. Through journaling, solitude, and prayer, I realized that God was wooing me away to spend more time with Him.

Several issues were rising to the surface.

CHAPTER 6
REFUELING AND REBUILDING

IN THE SPRING OF 2013, I stepped away from the singles class and attended a later church service. While awkward at first, sitting alone proved to be an advantage. As I worshipped God, I was free to close my eyes and lift my hands without others moving and talking around me. I had freedom to invite friends and coworkers to church, since I wasn't committed to the 9:00 a.m. service, 10:45 class, and 12:30 lunches. Attending the later service also provided time before church to read in my Bible and to journal. By the time I arrived for the service, my heart and mind were tuned in to God, ready to worship.

That is when my inner healing journey began. I strayed from traditional medicine and consulted a holistic wellness doctor that a church friend had recommended. Since my twenties I had used prescription medications to control adult acne, but I had stopped using them after seeing a law-firm advertisement discussing serious side effects. I prayed the acne wouldn't return, but it did.

The wellness doctor started me on the Candida diet after a diagnosis of leaky gut syndrome. It's a common ailment, but most cases are undiagnosed. Our current medical system doesn't recognize it as a health condition because it doesn't fit their model of symptom diagnosis and pharmaceutical treatment. Wellness doctors heal the immune system ("gut") with natural supplements, diet, and lifestyle changes.

So, what exactly caused my gut to "leak?" High stress levels, anxiety, and birth-control pills (used to treat my acne) caused tiny tears in my intestinal lining. These tears caused food particles to leak into my bloodstream after every meal, triggering an immune

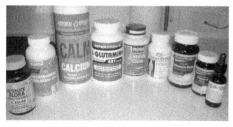

overdrive response that eventually led to food allergies and an autoimmune disease. A blood test revealed that I was allergic to gluten, dairy, yeast, eggs, whey, almonds, mushrooms, cranberries, kidney beans, and sesame seeds! In order to heal my gut, which was the root cause of my acne, my diet *had* to change. I eliminated all of the allergens, as well as foods that fueled Candida yeast growth, while adding natural supplements to repair my intestinal lining.

It was difficult cutting out all those foods *and* sugar, starches, and grains in order to reduce inflammation in my body. Forbidden foods also included: fruit, carrots, corn, rice, potatoes, pasta, bread, chips, salad dressings, condiments, coffee, tea, and alcohol. My list of restrictions was *3 times longer* than the list of foods I could eat! I pressed heavily into God through prayer because I needed His strength daily to stay on course. New habits ensued, along with a new grocery store and new recipes. No more frozen dinners!

A beautiful parallel of dual healing happened—as I pressed into God for physical healing, He revealed issues in my heart and mind that needed spiritual healing. I had sinful patterns of thinking and behaving that were rooted in false beliefs, and they had become second nature: self-pity, anger, frustration, and rejection. As I prayed, the Lord showed me the origin. My self-worth and self-image were damaged in my childhood. He showed me that anger was my way of dealing with hurt and disappointment. Frustration came from unmet expectations and attempts to control my circumstances. Self-pity resulted from feeling unworthy, and rejection was the thread that tied them all together. (I share more about this revelation in Part II.)

Slowly my soul began to heal through journaling and confessing my sin. I completed a mind-renewing study guide at night and listened to the corresponding teachings driving to and from work.

I meditated on twelve Biblical principles, reciting them out loud throughout the day. I had long, honest conversations with God while sitting outside admiring the nature He created—like the beautiful trees, birds, clouds, and sunsets.

Life slowed down dramatically to make time for this one-on-one counseling session with the Creator of the universe. I rearranged my priorities, and time with God trumped social gatherings. He pruned off friends who lacked the time or interest in developing a consistent friendship. Some repeatedly cancelled our plans, while others ignored my attempts to connect. It was a continuous cycle of disappointments, one after the other, after the other. I prayed about how to proceed.

The Holy Spirit nudged me to put my friends on the "altar of sacrifice." I visualized walking each friend to the cross, laying them down, and walking away. God would either resurrect the friend, returning them to me with a phone call, text, or email, or they would stay silent at the altar. The friends who did not reach out to me were the ones I needed to let go of. With the Spirit's help, I forgave each one for not loving me. It was hard to release friends that I cared about, but I trusted God to replenish my circle. *The Lord gives and the Lord takes away. Blessed is the name of the Lord!*

In addition to losing friendships, there were challenges at work, where the Lord guided me to stand firm and not to retreat. He walked me through my fears, one day at a time, training me to respond out of my *new nature* and not my old. I clung to Scripture when lies flooded my mind. Over and over, I stood against fears in my mind while doing my job at the office. I probably appeared "sane" on the outside, but inside there was a raging battle of good versus evil, God versus Satan. Strongholds in my mind were under attack, and the roots ran decades deep.

This season of rebuilding was critical to continuing my journey with Jesus. It was during that time that my prayer life took root. Lies were exposed and truth was revealed. Sins were confessed and mercy was granted. The more I healed, the more God used me to show His love and forgiveness to others. My health, relationships, and workplace trials were all valuable opportunities to strengthen my dependence on Him.

My journey of healing does not end here but continues to this day. And it will continue until the time when the Lord calls me home to heaven. I have learned that pain and progress are to be shared for the purpose of helping others in their time of suffering. God does not waste anything. If we are willing to humble ourselves and bring Him our hurts, He will heal us in due time. But *as we wait* for healing, God wants to use us to comfort others with the eternal hope of Jesus Christ.

In the next part of the book, you will see me walk through the healing process. My daily journal entries uncover how God has repeatedly used painful circumstances to accomplish His divine purposes in me and through me. I am reminded of Romans 8:28 as stated in the New Living Translation: "And we know that God causes everything to work together for the good of those who love God and are called according to his purpose for them." Ultimately, hardships are for our *good* and for His *glory*, transforming us closer into His loving image.

PART II

THE ACTION SCENES

Part II

Introduction

THE FIRST PART OF this book was an "aerial view" of my testimony of faith in Jesus Christ. This next section zooms in to the "action scenes," using some of my daily journal entries from 2001 to 2015. My inner thoughts and struggles are exposed to show the evolution of my transformation over time. As you read, you will travel with me through my past and experience my transition from a nonbeliever to a church attender, to a believer in Jesus, and then to a follower of Christ—one step at a time.

Look for God's fingerprints throughout these pages: answered prayers, miracles, exposed sin, and trials. He used various people and circumstances to draw me closer to His kingdom. He was at work in my struggles and in my victories. Through it all, God orchestrated *every* detail. To His name be all honor, glory, and praise! Amen.

(If you missed the NOTES BEFORE TAKEOFF at the front of this book, please go back and review them before continuing.)

MOST FREQUENTLY RECURRING NAMES

Abbreviations and Groups
CGC – financial services employer
CSA – Christian Single Adults dating network
DFW – Dallas/Fort Worth
IBC – Irving Bible Church
IPC – Integrated Physics and Chemistry
Single Impact – church singles class
Synergy – Sunday school class
Thrive – church singles group
TWU – Texas Woman's University

Female Friends
Amanda – oil painting, Fellowship Church
Amy – high school friend, Michigan
Amy – Lincoln Electric training
Cheri – home team leader, Fellowship Church
Christie – ski trip, Fellowship Church
Dana – neighbor in Lewisville
Erica – The Village Church
Jasmine – Irving Bible Church
Lisa – college study buddy, Michigan
Lucy – coworker, Irving Bible Church
Marie – first Dallas friend
Nancy – mentor, Irving Bible Church
Nisa – high school friend, Michigan
Pat – coworker
Renee – childhood friend, Michigan
Shannon – Dr. Leaf conference
Steff – college study buddy, Michigan
Terri – realtor, Irving Bible Church
Wendy – home team friend, Fellowship Church

Male Friends
Alex – dated from eHarmony
Ben – acquaintance from church
Clay – Lincoln Electric training
Danny – welding salesman, spiritual dad
David – dated from church
Derek – dated from church
Dong – spin class, Irving Bible Church
Edward – student teaching mentor
Eric – dated before my salvation
Henry – third Christian boyfriend
Jake – dreamboat from Chicago, dated before my salvation
James – second Christian boyfriend
Jim – work acquaintance and flirt
José – ski trip, Fellowship Church
Ken – married coworker
Kevin – boyfriend before my salvation
Luke – first Christian boyfriend
Mike – fourth Christian boyfriend
Paul – acquaintance from church
Pete – work acquaintance and flirt
Scott – crush from church
Tim – eHarmony match
Todd – dated before my salvation
Tom and Sue – married couple, Irving Bible Church
Warren – welding salesman, spiritual dad

Spiritual Mentors
Dr. Caroline Leaf – cognitive neuroscientist, speaker, and author
Dr. Tony Evans – pastor, speaker, and author
Joyce Meyer – author, speaker, and practical Bible teacher

Chapter 7

Life before Death

MY GRANDMOTHER'S WOODEN CHEST has been in my possession since I graduated college. One January night in 2016, I carefully retrieved twelve of my precious journals from inside. They contained thoughts and memories from my early twenties through age thirty-seven. As I relived moments of my past captured on paper, I was surprised to discover occasional references to God, which I can only attribute to my mother's influence and one or two friends. Growing up without church or a Bible, I believed in God but had no clue who His Son was.

This chapter begins with the year leading up to my salvation. My lifestyle and priorities before accepting Jesus Christ as Lord and Savior were different than they were after accepting Him. The following entries reflect who I was at the age of twenty-four and what was occurring in my life at that time.

[ONE YEAR BEFORE MY SALVATION]

July 27, 2001 [A New Start]

I'm on my new couch, writing in this new journal. It's appropriate that I have this new beginning, because Kevin and I are starting our lives as single people. Last Sunday, I invited him over to talk. I was feeling uncherished and unloved; I decided we aren't soulmates and I suggested a one-month break with no contact, but he suggested we still hang out.

This week was crazy—a visitor from headquarters was with me for 3 days. I stayed at the office Wednesday until 8:00 p.m., Thursday I was at an end-user's plant until 8:30 p.m., and tonight, I got home close to 7:00 p.m. I'm worn out! Since Lincoln is down in sales, we have to work every Saturday.

August 5, 2001

I'm ready for bed after a 3-day weekend in San Antonio. I met my new niece—so precious!

This is the second weekend since we had "the talk." I haven't spoken with Kevin since he came over for ice cream. Marie said I shouldn't be too available since we aren't dating. She's probably right.

I went back to Christian Single Adults. It felt strange to walk in as a single woman, just like two years ago. I flipped through binders and no one caught my eye. I felt depressed, because I don't want to pick anyone; I want someone to pick me. Something tells me that I'm not going to meet Mr. Right through CSA. **I will put my faith in the Lord to bring my prince when the time is right.** It's comforting to know the perfect one for me is out there!

August 18, 2001 [Dating God's Way?]

Marie and I went back to CSA, and my profile is now "back in the binder." I'm reading *I Kissed Dating Goodbye*, the book Renee gave me a year ago. It focuses on the road to righteousness and putting your trust in God. There are some challenging suggestions, such as limiting interactions with guys and avoiding one-on-one situations. Basically, don't date, don't flirt, and don't spend time looking for love. Well, that contradicts the whole CSA theory.

Six guys picked my profile, but I'm more interested in having friends. I said yes to four of them. Funny, one of my ex-buddies picked my profile! He dumped me in December, the night before my company's bonus dinner! It was almost two years ago. I have no desire to reconnect after the way he treated me.

Last week, I emailed my Michigan friends and my brother about the breakup. I wrote my parents a note and feel ashamed for not telling them over the phone. They like Kevin so much. Mom has framed pictures all over the house. Down they go.

Kevin came over Sunday to watch *The Practice*. It was only awkward in the beginning. He's a better listener now, but our relationship was always fundamentally flawed. I'm strong with my decision to separate. **The Lord has given me strength.** I should have done this a year ago. Looking back, there are many instances where he conveyed his lack of respect.

August 24, 2001

Another work week finished. I spoke with two guys from CSA; one was obnoxious. The very first thing he said was, "What are you doing this weekend?" I was dumbfounded! What nerve! He continued blabbing about himself. After 30 minutes, I had had it! I spoke for five minutes! I ended the conversation, telling him to call me later. I rang Marie right away to laugh about this "psycho profiler" who wants to go back to school for twelve more years!

August 28, 2001

Last night at the gym, I talked to a recruiter from e-Models. I was invited to a session in Dallas, but I don't know if I can make it. I'll be golfing that morning and then at a service call in Ft. Worth.

Tomorrow I'll be in Weatherford and Mineral Wells. My customer Wayne wants me to call when I'm driving through. One of these days, he wants to teach me how to shoot a gun.

August 31, 2001 [Locked and Loaded]

Wayne and I met after my calls in Mineral Wells. We bought bullets and a hunting license at Gibson's and drove to his friend's house. The 3 of us sat up front in the pickup, with me in the middle. Chad is a hoot! He asked, "Where are you from?" "Are those your real eyes?" "How old are you?" "How tall are you?" "Do you have kids?" After I answered his questions, he belted, "Shit, Wayne! You gotta marry this girl!" When Chad heard my parents live in Michigan, he said, "Oh, Wayne! You should marry her—her parents live far away!"

We had a few beers and drove to Chad's property outside of town. They taught me how to shoot a gun! I started out with a 9mm (I think) semiautomatic. The first trigger-pull scared me and I jumped. I shot several more times, missing my target until the very end.

September 4, 2001

Kevin and I saw *Rush Hour 2*. Things are going well for him, except that his company released more pilots. It doesn't look possible for him to make it into the "right seat." I mean the "left seat" (the captain's chair). He's thinking about going to a new airline.

I'm still reading *I Kissed Dating Goodbye*. It communicates the need for singles not to date, but to spend time with friends doing activities. I don't know if I can isolate myself to that extent. **God is supposed to be my focus, but dating is why I joined CSA.**

September 7, 2001

I'm not in the best mood. For one, I'm drunk because of an incident this afternoon. I went to meet Wayne and Chad at Fox and Hounds. Chad made fun of my red eyes ("Are you smoking marijuana?") and then teased me because I don't have many friends in Dallas. I haven't seen many movies, and therefore I've been "locked in a closet," which explains why I am the way I am. Chad made comments about our waitress and then asked if it had been a while since I "did it!" I was so offended that I almost cried in the restroom. I lasted 30 seconds before I excused myself and left.

Wayne called me on my mobile and at home. The fifth time he called, I was drunk enough on Jack Daniels to answer. We talked for fifteen or twenty minutes. He needed to fix something to eat and said he'd call me back. That was over an hour ago. I'm still a bit drunk and getting pissed. I get frustrated because he's inconsiderate. He says he'll call and doesn't. I'm very close to calling and bitching him out.

Okay, I left a message that I didn't appreciate waiting around for him to call me back. It's rude!

September 8, 2001

I'm feeling better. Not as angry, but still disappointed. Wayne left a message claiming he called my house phone and kept receiving an "AT&T message." He said he'd call today but hasn't. I'm struggling with anger, and yet I know I'm overreacting; he takes nothing seriously, and I take things personally. I felt great all week and now I'm pulling myself together. I don't want to talk to him, but still I expect him to call. Something tells me he won't. I probably ended it by leaving that voice mail, but I wasn't finished with our conversation. I had more to get off my chest.

Ok, it's almost 2:00 a.m. . . . (Still no word from Wayne; I made a mistake by leaving that message. *Mars and Venus on a Date* says to never call a man when you're upset. I blew it.)

September 9, 2001
It goes to show, the female mind overreacts. I called Wayne to apologize for my nasty message. I hadn't heard from him and thought he was mad at me. Turns out, he wasn't mad. He was dove hunting, so we didn't talk long. Wayne said he would take me dove hunting sometime. That would be fun.

September 13, 2001 [The Day America Changed]
Two days ago, on 9/11/01, terrorists attacked America. Two United Airlines flights were hijacked and flown into the World Trade Center in New York—the Twin Towers. One plane hit the first tower, over one hundred stories tall, at 8:50 a.m., and the other hit the second tower twenty-five minutes later. All people on board died. The death toll is approximately 3 thousand. An American Airlines flight was hijacked and crashed into the Pentagon an hour later. Initial reports claim that at least 3 hundred people died inside the Pentagon. It is presumed the White House was the intended target. Another airline was hijacked and crashed into a field southeast of Pittsburgh. All on board died.

The news is broadcasting twenty-four hours a day. Osama Bin Laden is the suspected mastermind from Afghanistan. This attack has been compared to Pearl Harbor, except that military people died there. Here, innocent civilians and government officials were killed. It's hard to turn off the TV.

I talked to Kevin yesterday; he and his family are all right. Two of the hijacked planes left the Boston airport where he has been many times. Officials identified eighteen hijackers and are tracing them back to the places they stayed and the rental cars they drove.

So much chaos and so much pain, it's hard to think about anything else. The nights go slowly. When I return from work, I look forward to sleeping to escape the grim reality of what happened. Even at the gym, all the TVs have news coverage and images.

In honor of the victims, I mounted a small American flag on my balcony.

September 16, 2001

Things are busier at work. One week of sales calls, one week of setup, and then one week of distributor training coming up. The week after, I drive to San Antonio to work an open house. I'll stay with my brother and family; Mom and Dad will also be in town. It'll be a nice break.

I spoke with Wayne. Things aren't going well and he quit his job. I won't see him much, and that might be for the best.

September 24, 2001 [Giving God Credit]

Well, God has been good to me this year—I'm up in sales 30 percent! (My goal was 8 to 10 percent). On the flip side, it will be tough to beat next year.

Although I was stressed earlier, I feel peaceful at the moment. Maybe it's because I'm alone after hosting weekend visitors; maybe it's because I stayed late at the office and feel more on top of things; maybe it's because I hear the clock ticking as I relax. . . .

September 26, 2001

I got home around 9:30 p.m. If all goes well (please, please), I will sell forty inverter welding packages.

Kevin has been silent for weeks. I called Wayne today. He's back to welding but wants to sell his machine. I hope he'll call me in a few days (like he said he would). I enjoy talking to him.

October 2, 2001 [Asking God for Help]

I called Kevin back and left a message. I want my spare key and bathing suit. I also want to know why he didn't call. Wayne barely calls. I know God has a plan for me, and I'm not worried. Wayne isn't my type, but he's the only one I think about. I'm better off if I don't think about him.

Lord, please help me stay focused.

October 21, 2001 [Up on the Bar]

The past month was challenging—many late nights, early mornings, and numerous all-day welding events on my feet.

Marie took me out for dinner in honor of my birthday. We went to Chow Thai in Addison, and I liked the atmosphere, food, and drinks. I tried a Kamikaze—it was super!

Saturday, I met coworkers at Cowboys Red River and danced with two guys (two-step). I went up on the bar with six girls and danced. We made it on their TV screen for four minutes. It was fun!

My manager discussed my performance, rating me a 130 out of 160. I was in second place for total new stick electrode business during the promotion, but since the terrorist attack, our sales have dropped. I was down 13 percent in September.

October 28, 2001 [Men, Music, and Drinks]

Marie and I went to CSA and then ate dinner at Cuba Libre. It was our first time—very trendy, attractive people, and a DJ spinning house music. We went to Sipango's, where a band played seventies and eighties music. Across the street, we checked out Samba Room—full of guys. Then we went dancing in Greenville. We had a fun night and tried four new places!

I said yes to two guys at CSA: Oliver and Eric.

All in all, I'm living it up this month! For the weekend record, I consumed: one Long Island iced tea, two beers, 3

Jack and Cokes, two glasses of wine, and two frozen drinks!
And water!

November 4, 2001

Eric and I had a great conversation over dinner. The time flew!
We have the same sense of humor and talked about sledding,
skiing, movies, and family cars. He walked me to my door and
gave me a hug.

I went to CSA and said yes to meeting Todd. That same
day he called to invite Marie and me to join him and his friend
from Cleveland. They met us at 10:30 p.m. outside Samba
Room. We sat at a table having drinks until 1:00 a.m. and then
went to Rio Room. We were shocked when it was "last call."
Todd's looking for friends too, and has been in Dallas four
months. I hope we get to know each other. He's much cuter
than his picture.

Kevin may stop by Thursday to deliver my key and swim
suit. He doesn't call anymore, but I'm so busy it doesn't
matter. At least Eric's interested in me! I just wish I would
stop thinking about Todd.

November 11, 2001 [Stained by Sin]

Here was my week:

Monday—dinner and drinks with customers
Tuesday—dinner in Deep Ellum and Stained concert with
distributors [We thought we had tickets to see Sting!]
Wednesday—dinner date with Eric
Thursday—talked to Todd and Eric
Friday—dinner with Todd and then drinks in Greenville.

I paid the twenty-dollar cover for both of us (he's looking
for friends and I offered). After our drink, Todd was ready to
dance. I was drunk and loved the music. Not long thereafter,
we started kissing. We had another drink on the loveseat near
the bar. Our arms were around each other and we kissed some
more. After more dancing, we drove to his place. I made sure

we didn't go all the way, and told him at one point that we'd
have to stop. He said that was all right. We fell asleep and I
woke up several times in the night, getting only four hours of
sleep. This was my first time staying the night with a guy I wasn't
seriously dating. This was our second date! I didn't think it
would go so far, but now that we've "crossed the line," I don't
know how things will be. We are both dating other people, and
I don't want to be intimate with more than one person. Things
are confusing enough.

(I share details in this journal because I can't confide this to
anyone.) Like my mother, I keep personal and private things
to myself. **I won't even tell my best friend, since Renee is
so pure and Christian.** She'd be disappointed. The sad part is
that I enjoyed dancing and making out with Todd. I felt sexy
and powerful. I don't remember feeling that way ever before.

Since turning twenty-five, I feel like a new person—young,
single, and having the time of my life! Kevin seemed to bring
me down. Since he and I split, I'm having fun with customers
and drinking more. My sales are up. I'm experiencing more of
Dallas: new bars, new restaurants, and new guys!

November 16, 2001

Tonight is Friday and I'm staying in. I thought Todd may be
available for a movie, but his parents called while we were
on the phone. I don't know why I'm paranoid. I look at Todd
and see an ex-frat boy who has probably dated many girls. We
have a lot in common and can talk forever, *but* since we took
things to a "higher level" so soon, I'm leery he won't stick
around. That's what those girl/guy books say—give up too
much too soon and the man will lose interest. I'm worried he
will.

Amy from high school sent me a birthday gift, a Snoopy
journal! It's great, because I'm halfway done with this one. I
write more frequently now than in past years; I guess I have

more time for self-reflection. **It feels good to empty my thoughts on paper and go to bed.**

November 29, 2001 [Opening Up]
Last week was Thanksgiving and I spent five days in Troy. I got to chat with Renee for a couple of hours before the feast. My brother and family were also in town. Saturday night my parents treated me to dinner at Charlie's Crab. We split two bottles of wine, and I opened up about my dating life. They seemed not only interested, but happy!

Eric came over last night to cook dinner. If Marie stays in town, we might go dancing. Now Todd, who knows what's up with him? Marie said to sit back and let Todd lead. That's fine if we are dating, but I don't know what we are, other than two strangers who got drunk and messed around. If we had kept things "normal," then he may be interested in pursuing. It bothered me that he didn't open any of the doors. That's why I thought it may not be a true date, but he paid for dinner and drinks. I don't think he knows how to make a lady feel special ("the Kevin Syndrome"). **Why are women attracted to guys who look fine but lack the ability to make them feel cherished and appreciated?**

9:05 p.m.
Eric sent flowers! A beautiful bouquet of white roses, pink carnations, daisies, and lilies!

December 4, 2001
Today is Tuesday. I had a good workout, but I noticed more fat on my arms and stomach. It's been over two weeks since I went to the gym; I have five to ten pounds to lose.

Todd called Sunday and wants to go dancing again. It's been four weeks!

Marie and I talked about Todd's behavior. I feel torn; I like him but am unsure how much he likes me. On the other hand,

Eric really likes me and I'm unsure of my feelings. If Todd weren't in the picture, I may have feelings for Eric. I've never dated this many guys at once! [There were 3 in total.] **I may be headed down the path of self-destruction—trying to spread myself too thin.**

December 9, 2001

Todd picked me up Friday and we drove to Greenville. It wasn't as fun this time because he was tired. He took me home and came inside to use my bathroom. I played my James album and the Alice in Chains song, "Don't Follow." By 3:00 a.m., we started kissing on my couch. Todd left at 4:30 a.m. and I crashed in bed. I drank too much. I woke up with ringing ears and a dry mouth.

We seem to be "casual kissing friends." My strong attraction lessens the more I get to know him. Marie doesn't like Todd because of the things I've told her (less the intimate details). She thinks I'm weak for not giving him the boot.

December 15, 2001

Bonus day was Friday and my rating was higher than expected! Sadly, our company didn't reach our goal, so I made less money than last year.

December 22, 2001

I'm back in Troy for Christmas. Last week, Todd and I caught *Vanilla Sky* with Tom Cruise—kind of weird. It makes me think about how important every minute of our lives is. **At any moment, we can make a decision that will change our lives forever—in a good way or a terrible way.**

January 1, 2002 [First Christmas Service]

Happy New Year! I'm at Detroit Wayne Metro waiting for my flight back to Dallas. My ten days in Troy are over. Steff [from college] and I bowled 3 games; I won all 3 and got my *first* "turkey"—3 strikes in a row!

My parents and I attended church on Christmas Eve for the first time. On New Year's Eve, I went to Clutch Cargo's with Nisa [from high school]. It had different music and a different crowd. We had fun, but it wasn't the best time—a $30 cover, and the guys were unattractive!

January 14, 2002

All this solitude is a bit too much. I stayed in all weekend to rest from my cold. Eric and I wished each other well [after I told him that I don't want a steady relationship].

I'm struggling with thoughts about Todd. **The mind is a powerful thing. It can play all sorts of tricks on you. It can make you see things that aren't there. It can make you believe things that are not true.** I guess it's the fault of the imagination.

January 18, 2002

It's Saturday, past midnight. I wanted to clear my head before turning in. It's been a week since I left a message for Todd, two weeks since I last saw him. I called again today. My guess is something has changed in his life—did he meet someone new? Maybe he lost interest (ouch!). Whatever it is, I must be strong. I was weak to call him.

Women blame themselves when things like this happen. We feel as though we drove him away. Although I acknowledge that I'm a wonderful person with much to give, it's hard to cut off the attachment. I think of Todd whenever the phone rings. That will pass. **Rejection stings no matter who you are or how long you've known someone.** I met Todd 3 months ago and it lasted longer than I expected.

O Romeo, O Romeo, where art thou?

January 26, 2002 [First Visit to Fellowship Church]
> I had a stressful week at work—everything happening at once!
> Marie and I met for dinner and drinks last night. She took
> me to Fellowship Church tonight for the Saturday 6:30 p.m.
> service. The church is huge and looks like an office building.
> It has stadium seating and an overhead balcony to fit all the
> people. The topic was "Body by God," focusing on diet,
> exercise, and caring for our bodies. I enjoyed it a lot.

February 3, 2002 [Romeo Arrives!]
> I almost wrote in this journal yesterday, but something told me
> to wait until Sunday. I had the most amazing night last night!
> I worked the Tru-Serve show with a coworker and picked him
> up at 10:00 p.m. to join several male vendors at The Bone in
> Deep Ellum. Jake is from Chicago, 30 years old, and over six
> feet tall. We talked a few times, but he didn't seem interested
> in me.
>
> [Later in the evening] Jake and I danced in the Red Room
> at Club Clearview and then cooled off outside. Who knows
> how long we walked, but we lost track of time and he lost his
> glasses! After searching on Main Street, we headed to my car
> at 3:00 a.m. and talked for an hour.
>
> Jake is a very beautiful person who makes people laugh. He
> complimented my height, my hair, and my eyes—and asked
> me out for dinner, "just you and me." I drove him to his hotel
> and we stood outside talking. "Now I'm going to kiss you" he
> said with a smile. He stepped in, cupped my face, and kissed
> me. It was an ending from a movie! Everything Jake did was
> perfect. (He put Kevin and Todd to shame.)
>
> I'm trying to stay grounded because he lives in Chicago.
> He returns to Dallas for another hardware show in March. But
> then what? First, let's see if he calls. It seems too good to be
> true! Jake seems too good to be true!

Dear God, please let me hold on to my heart with this one! I can't take my mind off him. I replay the events over and over. The way he looked at me and smiled.

February 5, 2002

Early morning, and I can't sleep. Jake made reservations at the Palomino in the Crescent Hotel. It was a very nice place. He asked for the best table, quiet and private. I ate the salmon (which he ordered for me) and he had the tuna. The evening was amazing. We talked for over an hour before we ordered! We shared our dreams for the "ideal future." He wants a family someday, as do I. Jake plays in a 3-man band and . . . I could go on and on. He treated me like a lady again.

Around 11:40, we parted ways. Jake said he'd call sometime to let me know he's alive. He thanked me for making his trip to Dallas memorable—"one that will not be easily forgotten." He asked if I'd like to have dinner the next time he comes to town. Of course I said yes. Pinch me—I'm dreaming!

Thank you, God, for the strength you gave me yesterday, and please help me stay focused. Jake's like no other that I have known. Take care of him.

February 10, 2002

Good Morning! In case you were wondering, Jake flew out Tuesday and called on Wednesday. We spoke for 3 minutes because we were working. He thanked me again for dinner and said, "I'm looking forward to seeing you in March."

I called Mom and told her that I met "this amazing guy" and "I think he's The One." I started crying. What if he is?

February 21, 2002 [Presidential Praise]

Well, the 2002 ARA Rental Show is behind us. I'm at the New Orleans airport waiting for my flight to Dallas. I sold a lot of equipment and received a $10,000 order from my Fort Worth customer! Our national rental manager was impressed.

The president and vice president of Lincoln Electric were also there. The president walked up to me and said, "I have to tell you that you do a wonderful job on your weekly reports. I read all of them and very few stand out. Yours are some of the best." A few hours later, he said to the vice president, "She's the one who does the best job on those weekly reports." I smiled and said he could put a smiley face on my next one if he wanted. All 3 of us laughed. I hope that means the president likes me. He's hard to impress.

A group of Lincoln coworkers went to Bourbon Street. After two Hurricanes and two beers, I was pushed on stage. I had a Bud Light in one hand and a microphone in the other; the man in the white suit had me sing "I Will Survive" by Gloria Gaynor. It's ironic how I sang karaoke to that song four years ago when I came here with Steff and Lisa [during spring break in college]! I did it solo! Oh, the magic of Bourbon Street!

February 25, 2002

Time for a new game plan, I haven't heard from "him." His knee surgery is tomorrow, and I thought he'd call today. I must stop thinking about Jake. No more trance music in the car; it's too much of a reminder. I'm not throwing in the towel, but I have to reroute my thinking.

Lord, please give me strength to refocus and trust all the goodness that you will provide.

March 9, 2002

Next week is the Ace Hardware Show. This means that, theoretically, Jake should call to reserve me in advance. That is, if he's still interested. I could have sworn he was head-over-heels (maybe not "in love"). The next few weeks will reveal the truth.

Please, Lord, help me be strong and stay focused.

March 17, 2002

Sunday. I went to Fellowship Church alone this morning because Marie cancelled on me. I really wanted to go, so I did. The sermon hit home—"Impossible Possibilities." The pastor explained how we try to control our circumstances; and when we face a seemingly impossible situation, we need to give it to God. Let Him solve it and don't rush Him to fit our schedule.

That's what I've been guilty of, wanting to hurry things along with Jake. Whether he calls or not, I can't control. I must live my life, and if he comes around, fine. If not, oh well. **I must put my faith in God and let Him navigate through life's journey.** I will continue to pray for strength in my thoughts and actions. I pray for the moment that God decides I'm ready for my soulmate.

March 21, 2002 [Where Art Thou, Romeo?]

What's wrong here? It's 3:35 a.m. and I can't sleep! This is the 3rd night in a row. Jake is in town, and I'm uneasy. He called Tuesday to say he's coming, and he'll call again on Wednesday. Yesterday came and went. I know he's interested, but maybe he's afraid of calling too much. I'm excited to talk to him—and see him. That's why I'm writing—to clear my head!

Marie and I haven't spoken since last week. She didn't go to church with me.

Just now I said a prayer for strength to make it through the open house from hell (kidding)—and to remain patient and faithful about my situation with Jake. I don't want to force or control things.

March 23, 2002

I called Jake from the open house and he invited me out with him and my coworker. We met at the Magnolia Hotel, and then headed to Deep Ellum. Jake and I danced again on stage at Club Clearview. It was fun! We stayed out until 2:00 a.m. and took a taxi back to his hotel. I was buzzing.

I slept in Jake's bed, and he behaved himself wonderfully. We did no more than kiss, cuddle, and talk. He's an amazing person. **Jake makes me feel like the most beautiful woman.** He has this way of looking at me, deep in thought, studying my face and smiling to himself.

The next morning, he showed me his scars from surgery and handed me the TV remote. Five minutes later, he surprised me with a cup of hot coffee and put it on the nightstand. He brought creamer and sugar and then went to shower. What a sweetheart! When it was time to leave, he waited with me for the valet. Jake kissed me, and then again when I dropped him off at the convention center.

March 27, 2002

I saw Jake a few times at the Ace Hardware Show, and he surprised me with an apple and bottled water. Earlier, he called to see if I was there; I guess he was excited to see me.

That evening we drove to Lombardi's in the West End, a trendy Italian restaurant. Jake made reservations, and we had a nice table by the window. Everything was going well until he mentioned the distance between Chicago and Dallas. It felt like he was giving reasons why it won't work to maintain our relationship. I fell quiet as my heart sank. He noticed I was unhappy.

"Did I say too much?"

"Yes."

"Are you mad at me?"

"No."

"What then? Please tell me."

"I guess it wasn't what I wanted to hear."

I tried to explain without putting my heart on the table. We moved past it, but he sent an email yesterday that touched on our "finite" situation and how we agreed we'd live our lives and carry on. My heart sank again. Am I overreacting? Or is my gut trying to tell me something? He is dating someone in Chicago, but it doesn't sound serious. He has a huge crush on me (his words).

We walked outside holding hands and stopped at T.G.I. Friday's for more beers. We talked a lot—music, religion, etc. Jake doesn't consider himself to be Christian or religious. I was surprised and disappointed; my mom would be crushed. **Is this a test from God? Or is my role to teach Jake and share the love and teachings of the Lord?**

We drove back to his hotel around 12:30 a.m. and valeted my car for the night. Things stayed manageable. I left the next morning and Jake worked the show. We kissed farewell, and he called me later that day. I met him one last time before he left. We held hands, and I was nervous. He thanked me for everything, saying "Parting is such sweet sorrow," and I'll hear from him "sooner rather than later."

I read his email and responded. I didn't mention how the second paragraph made me feel— sad. I tried to be light and airy like everything was fine. I had mixed feelings and reread it several times. I need to stop analyzing. What will be, will be.

April 8, 2002

I talked to Jake today and 3 days ago. It's wonderful to hear his voice—better than his emails! He told me that he misses me. It was a very vivid moment. I was parked at my apartment when he whispered, "I miss you. In no way, shape, or form am I exaggerating in the least when I say that I miss you."

April 19, 2002

Jake mailed the picture of us in Deep Ellum along with a CD from his band. It's sexy knowing he wrote all the music and lyrics!

April 23, 2002

Life comes with ups and downs. My mood changes by the hour. Jake's email said he won't be coming in May, more like June. My mind screams, *Is June going to mean "June" or "July?"* His reasons are monetary and time frame. Earlier, he called our relationship doomed (indirectly), and now he's postponed his trip to Dallas! I guess have two choices:

1. Bitch like hell that reality is ruining my fantasy, or
2. **Sit back and let God take over.**

I must do the second option, but I don't know how to respond to his email. I don't want to be angry, but I am disappointed. I took down our picture and will store his CD away. He's not going to be my number one focus anymore.

May 3, 2002 [Parents Visit Fellowship]

Jake hasn't bought his airline ticket yet. I told him to tell me when he does.

Church is going well. I took my parents and they seemed to enjoy it. I enjoyed the past series on "Men and Women." Marie only made it to one of the four messages.

May 7, 2002

Up and down, back and forth—that's how it feels to be me. **Maybe it's intuition or paranoia, but I sense Jake has pulled back.** His emails are shorter and fewer. His response time has increased and my feelings change daily. I thought I was in love, but then he didn't write me Sunday or Monday (like usual) and my heart sank. I've grown too accustomed to our correspondence. Why do I feel that Jake won't make it down in June to see me?

May 24, 2002

Jake apologized for being "so sketchy lately" and told me how preoccupied he had been with work. He said that he is coming to Dallas but hasn't purchased a ticket. He was headed to the studio to finish their 3rd album.

I went to the 11:15 church service (alone) and met a lady while waiting in line for the restroom. She invited me to join her at the singles jazz picnic. It was fun!

May 27, 2002 [Close Encounter]

I'm on the plane to Dallas, leaving my parents and friends behind in Michigan. The weekend was very pleasant. Sunday, my parents and I stopped in Frankenmuth for dinner. What's crazy is when I called Nisa to tell her that we would stop by Grand Blanc to see her apartment, she was in Frankenmuth! Not only that, but she was only fifty feet away! Within minutes, she was standing in front of me!

I must get back to the gym and tanning beds to prep for my Florida trip! Work will be busy and so will my personal life. I'll let you know if Jake comes after all. It seems like forever since we spoke—at least 3 weeks!

June 1, 2002 [Moment of Truth]

WOW! The truth has been told—a new month, a new broken heart. (Rereading my previous entries, it seems this outcome has been building page after page.) Jake, the coward he is, has broken my heart via email. He is "semi-official" with a girl in Chicago. I received his email while I was in the office and started crying.

I printed his email and read it over and over. Each time, I picked up on a new sentence, a new meaning. Distance was the reason for casting me aside (my words). My favorite line: "Sorry for wavering, but I wasn't truly sure of anything myself until recently. Please be in touch. I certainly hope that you don't hate me. You're all class, Char, all class."

What do I do? My initial instinct was to do nothing—no response, ever—to write him off and let him live his life. I'm not against leaving Dallas, especially if I find my soulmate. **I**

prayed to God that He lead me on the path He has chosen.
The path probably leads away from Jake.

I've been awake since 6:00 a.m. and can't sleep. My mind swirled all night; I awoke with thoughts of Jake. I need advice from Renee and Nisa. I don't need Marie's, because she'll say, "Move on." Funny thing, it won't matter what I do, for God will determine the outcome. Should I let him know that he broke my heart? Should I tell him we may be soulmates?

June 2, 2002

My emotions are still swinging back and forth. I wrote my close friends an email yesterday explaining my heartbreak with Jake. I wish I could silence the voices inside my head. I haven't slept enough, and drinking alcohol the past two nights hasn't helped.

Please, God, give me strength and peace at this time in my life. Guide me in the direction that I should go. Mend my heart quickly.

June 3, 2002

Another day approaches its close. I felt weak and weary this morning but felt better once I got consumed at work with my training program.

Renee was right—Jake and I weren't reality-based. Our feelings were real, but not in the proper context. Part of me questioned his passion to become a rock star. I want a secure future for a family. It breaks my heart to imagine him gazing at another woman, but so be it. His feelings for me aren't strong enough to continue. I feel better today; no tears!

June 6, 2002

Today was not the best of days. Not bad, but not great. It felt as though my manager lectured me, and then my welding demo got cancelled.

This is the first time in a while that I've felt lonely. I left Marie a message. She has shown no support since I told her that Jake and I are over. We'll see if she calls back. I stopped asking her about church because she "never knows." I think she goes with her boyfriend but doesn't want me to know. I wonder when we'll see each other again.

June 9, 2002 [A Dangling Carrot]
Church was great—the final session was about self-esteem. Lord knows that I struggle with it, especially at work. Once I learn to stop comparing myself to my coworkers, then I can accept myself for who I am, faults and all! I did better last week and pray to keep it up!

Not to beat a dead horse, but I must drain out my thoughts about Jake. I was coping quite well, and then a strange thing happened: At 8:00 a.m. yesterday, my cell phone rang. I was in bed, wondering who would call that early on a Saturday! I went back to sleep and later checked my phone. It was an 847 area code. I listened to the message; they hung up after 3 seconds.

Jake's cell number has an 847 area code! It was someone from Chicago, no doubt. Maybe his girlfriend found my number? Did he call to hear my voice on the recording? This mystery may never be solved; I refuse to call the number.

June 10, 2002 [Feeling Faint]
Not a great day. I was at a manufacturing plant in Fort Worth when I became nauseous and light-headed. I sat down at the end of Bay 3 while someone got me some water. Several waves of nausea passed, and then I moved into the air-conditioning. I sat for ninety minutes in the front office. Was it stress or anxiety?

I've been thinking about Jake today—probably because of the phone call. I didn't think about him Saturday or Sunday, but today, yes. Part of me wants to call the number; should I?

I won't say anything. I could call during work hours and hopefully get an answering machine with a voice. Am I trying to torture myself? Do I really want him back? The best thing is to let go, and I thought I had.

Loneliness has fallen on my heart tonight. Surrounded by couples [at happy hour] didn't make me feel better. **I want to be patient with God's timing, but I don't understand why my life has been so hard lately.**

Please, God, give me peace and confidence to regain my old self again.

June 11, 2002 [Depression]

Okay, I think I have multiple personalities. I was doing well, but now I'm restless and sad. I've played the Jeff Buckley CD too many times. I feel hurt that Marie doesn't need me in her life and she doesn't return my calls. I don't want to give her the Michigan Mints anymore. That's why I called last week. She replied with an email saying to call her next week because she needs to check her schedule. What a crock of shit. I called her tonight while she was home, but no answer.

I hate to feel this way toward her—so evil and resentful. Shall I tell her? Shall I write her? I stopped asking her to church. I feel like I'm doing everything alone. Jake isn't there any longer for support and acceptance and Marie isn't there for me emotionally, mentally, or physically. I feel so restless.

I have felt that I should consider a new job. I don't feel like I belong in this welding world. What would I rather do? The economy has been so bad this year and finding employment is hard.

I feel depressed. What's wrong with me? I'm crying as I write this.

Please, God, give me strength and peace. I really need your help. I feel many things that I don't understand.

Chapter 8

Resurrected
at Fellowship Church

IT HAPPENED ON A Friday night in June, one or two weeks after receiving Jake's email. I wish I knew the exact date of my salvation, when I accepted Jesus Christ as my Lord and Savior. On that special night, I received the Holy Spirit and was born into the eternal family of God. I wish I had recorded this special moment in my journal, and yet I did not fully understand the significant impact of my decision until much later.

In this chapter, my long journey from brokenness to restoration begins. My old self dies and I am resurrected to a new life in Christ. As I learn to walk with Jesus over an eight-year period, my eyes and ears are opened. Sin is revealed, prayers are answered, and miracles occur. My heart and mind are gradually reformed through trials, obedience, God's grace, and the power of the Holy Spirit.

Let the transformation begin. . . .

[AFTER RECEIVING CHRIST AS MY LORD AND SAVIOR]

June 16, 2002

I saw Marie at church today with her secret boyfriend. She didn't see me and I was glad. I've talked to Renee about her, and she pointed out that whenever I mention Marie, it's been negative. She's right. Things got weird when I started dating Todd.

I want to leave Lincoln and leave welding. I wonder if my manager senses it. He spoke to me about "experiencing life as a single," job changes, and even modeling.

June 22, 2002

I'm on my way to Sanibel Island, Florida, to meet my family and Renee. I deleted Jake's cell number and filed his email in my letter box. No more reminders, no more rereading. Good-bye, good luck, and good riddance! I'm putting him 100 percent behind me.

Steff had a second miscarriage. Twice is considered bad luck, and 3 times is a sign that something is wrong. I pray that Steff and Ray will have a healthy baby when God says it's right.

I'm still confused about Marie and how I should handle myself. I gave her gift from Michigan (the mints) to my coworker and his wife.

July 17, 2002

Oil painting started last week and is enjoyable!

I confessed my job doubts to my boss. I try really hard, but don't feel I'm good at sales. I was crying on and off.

I feel better about it lately—my life. I don't think I'll be moving to Europe or New York. It was a fantasy, of course! The real journey I'm longing for is the journey to the center of my self—my very being. **I want to be in touch with who I am and what God wants me to become.**

August 9, 2002

Life is busy! I'm feeling better since my confession to my boss. I went to church last Saturday, where I ran into the lady from the jazz picnic. I called her earlier in the week, but she didn't call back.

My acne is flaring up. What causes acne? Why can't I get rid of it?

Oil painting is almost over. We are completing a snow scene. Mine came out well and the instructor said I have "nice brush strokes."

August 29, 2002

Breathe a sigh of relief—I'm on my way to Raleigh to see Renee and I'm on the plane. Words can't describe my excitement for this trip! At long last, it is here! Now I get to visit her world!

Last Saturday, I went to church with Amanda from painting class. Sunday was a home team barbeque. It was nice! I really like Wendy. We shared frustrations with work and how sensitive we are (i.e., crying in front of our bosses).

Work is going well because I have done a lot of praying about it. Long-term is the question. I pray this trip to Raleigh will help me find my path.

I researched pharmacy and chemistry careers. Am I willing to go back to school? That's two years plus summer internships and a big fat exam. If I can do chemical engineering, I can do this. If I can sell welding equipment, I can learn pharmacy. I'm blessed with many things; the ability to learn is one.

I'm also considering teaching. Teachers get summers off but don't make enough for what they do. But it's not supposed to be about the money. It's about fulfillment.

September 3, 2002 [First Christian Bookstore/Two Miracles]
My brother and sister-in-law celebrate another wedding anniversary—3 years!

My trip to Raleigh was great! [On my last day] Renee and I packed my bags and drove for frozen custard. We hit a Christian bookstore before the airport, and she gave me tips on how to choose a Bible. I'll buy one soon.

God did a wonderful thing when I arrived late at the airport. We lost track of time, and I was going to miss my flight. [I prayed to stay calm.] While standing in the [middle of a] long line for check-in, God sent an airline employee directly to me. He asked, "Curbside check-in?" [Confused, I stared at him.] "Can you print my boarding pass too?" "Yes," he replied, "come with me." *Within minutes*, my bag was checked and a boarding pass was in my hand, with fifteen minutes to go! I boarded in group one and was seated in bulkhead row 7, window seat, with extra leg room!

When I arrived in DFW, I realized that I lacked dollar bills to tip the shuttle driver. As I stood at baggage claim, I said to God, "Okay, the only way I'm going to ask for change for my ten-dollar bill is if you send someone directly to me. They can stand next to me, but they must be very close." *Within seconds*, a young man walked up and asked if I was familiar with Dallas. I gave him directions and made small talk. "Ask him for change," a small voice whispered. So I did. He had a five-dollar bill and five one-dollar bills! I was thrilled! ☺

I called Renee on my drive back to my apartment; she was excited too! [She had prayed that I would make my flight.] Unpacking my suitcase, I found her book *Fresh Wind, Fresh Fire* and her Jars of Clay CD! I love the CD [my first Christian album], and I've read a few pages in the book.

Home team meets at 6:30 tonight. I still need to buy a Bible and a notebook.

Wendy and I met at church for the First Wednesday service. It was good—music and communion. I'm thinking about joining the church soon. I don't know what's holding me back.

September 25, 2002 [First Break-In/First Bible]

My car window was smashed during the AWS meeting! Someone stole my briefcase by breaking the driver's window! I filed a police report and took my car to the repair shop. I miss my Maxima! I miss my Jars of Clay CD!

Last week I had lunch with Allan [welding customer]. We talked about church and the Lord, and he showed me his new Bible written in today's English. He met me Saturday at an open house to give me a New Living Translation Bible! He had said he would get me one like his. Well, what Allan had and what he bought were different. The receipt was in the bag, so I exchanged it for a smaller NLT Bible and paid an extra twenty-five dollars. I hope he won't mind. **A Bible is a very personal thing, not easily picked out by another.** I'm thankful for Allan and his generosity.

October 5, 2002

I had a grueling week with the Home Depot Tool Fair, end-user machine issues, and TruServ. I worked the show today, 8:00 a.m. to 6:00 p.m., and met several nice vendors. One introduced me as his fiancée! He's pretty cute. Home Depot had its own saga—a cute DeWalt rep kept staring at me.

Despite these prospects, I'm sad Jake didn't come by. I looked terrific—great hair day! God knows that I don't need him in my life, so why do I desire his attention? The past two shows he has been there. It's been four months since he broke my heart. He's moved on. Why do I feel let down? **God is protecting me from getting hurt again.** I shall be thankful for all that He has done.

October 26, 2002 [Forgiving One of Two]

I felt compelled to let Jake know that I have forgiven him. Since I erased his email address, I mailed a card to his band's fan club address. God will either deliver the note or it won't make it to him. Either way, let it be *His will*! **Too bad I can't find a peaceful way to forgive Marie.** We don't share much in common anymore, so I don't want to be friends. I wish she would move away so I won't see her again. Is that wrong? I want to wipe the slate clean from the people of my past and celebrate the new Charlotte!

November 3, 2002 [Stepping Out]

I told Mom about the Fellowship singles ski retreat in February 2003. I decided to take a leap of faith and go!

Yesterday I went to the home team retreat at Cedar Creek Lake. We sang worship songs, discussed our walk with Christ, and played games until 3:30 a.m.! It was fun.

November 6, 2002 [Heavy Heart]

Not a happy day, I must confess. I made mistakes at work and wanted to cry. I got home early, checked email, and then left for First Wednesday service. My home team was standing in a circle talking and I got a cheery "Hello!" and nothing more. Luke ignored me, Wendy came late, and I dropped my bread during communion; I was in a lousy mood. My back hurt, my singing was terrible, and Marie was seated a few rows away. I teared up twice and couldn't relax or pray. My heart remained sour. Why? I finished the Book of John last night and said my prayers, and yet I was disappointed in myself *all day*! **The voices of doubt and insecurity pulled me away from God.** A depression sank in my heart as I left church. What's the deal?

November 17, 2002 [Church Membership]

I attended the newcomer's class at Fellowship a week and a half ago. I decided that I'm ready to join the church; all I have to do now is get baptized. I plan to wait until the weather is warmer, since it is done outside.

November 24, 2002

The snow scene painting is complete but drying. I may give Dad the landscape instead.

The home team Thanksgiving potluck was tonight. I took pictures of my new friends and talked to Luke for a while. He suggested we play golf sometime.

Thank you, Lord, for a wonderful night of fellowship with awesome Christian friends! I love them!

November 27, 2002

Another trip awaits me this morning. I'm here at the gate for my flight to Troy. I'm so excited to see my family and friends! I shipped my painting [to Michigan for Dad's birthday] with lots of bubble paper. I prayed several times for God to watch over it.

November 30, 2002 [First Time Being Prayed Over]

I said the prayer [for the first time] before our family's Thanksgiving meal. I had practiced over and over until I memorized it. I was still a bit nervous.

A few nights earlier, at Metro [large single's gathering in Plano], they had those of us stand whose parents don't know Jesus. I stood up with only ten others. The pastor asked for those nearby to put a hand on us and pray out loud for our parents. When 3 home team friends prayed over me, **I felt my body temperature rise like a flame reaching my ears and radiating through my clothes.** It was either from embarrassment or the power of the Holy Spirit.

I haven't told my parents that I'm saved. They are accepting people, so I shouldn't be nervous. Mom will be happy and Dad won't care much. Hopefully it'll lead to a discussion, and yet I feel awkward.

UPS delivered the painting in one piece. (Thank you, God!) My parents loved it!

December 8, 2002 [Profession of Faith]

I told my parents that I accepted Jesus Christ as my Lord and Savior. Of course I wasn't as collected as I would've liked—I cried, practically sobbing during lunch. It weighed on my heart so heavily.

I confess to having pseudo-feelings for Luke. It's more of an external attraction than an inner connection. I felt uneasy at home team, more concerned about Luke than about God. Isn't that terrible? I have sinned. My mind imagines dating someone, and it becomes a mental fairy tale, not reality-based.

Please, God, help me focus on you. Don't let me be distracted by work or the activities of the season. Thank you for my church friends and support network. Please use me to do your will and lead me down the right path.

December 11, 2002 [First Christian Date]

I had a wonderful evening with Luke. He is a Christian man and was raised that way by his parents.

Thank you, God, for such an enjoyable evening with a guy who respects me for who I am. I hope we continue our friendship as we get to know each other. Let it be your will!

December 23, 2002 [The Dating Prayer]

Another year, another new journal. For Mom's birthday I gave her Charles Stanley's book, *Seeking His Face*. I hope she will keep up with the short daily readings.

I prayed today that God will direct me toward Luke, or away from Luke. I think he's falling for me. I have mixed feelings, because [even though I'm attracted to him] I approach dating differently than before I became a Christian. I see things more clearly and understand the power of a kiss.

December 25, 2002 [Saying Grace]

It's 7:00 p.m., after a pot-roast dinner in San Antonio. Luke called to wish me a Merry Christmas. My parents arrive in 3 days, and I'm excited about their gifts: photo ornaments, a Kinko's photo calendar, and a Bible for Mom (NLT, easier to read).

I said grace before dinner [with my family] the past two nights. Luke has wanted me to say grace on the past few dates, but I declined. The more I do it, the easier it is.

December 30, 2002

Back at the airport and my flight is delayed! I called Wendy to let her know, since she's meeting me at DFW. She saved me over $70 in parking!

Renee gave me a Christian rock worship CD from Third Day and a tape of a sermon from a guest speaker at her church in Raleigh.

January 2, 2003

Happy New Year! I spent half of New Year's Eve at the Fellowship party with my home team and the other half with Luke at a gathering in downtown Dallas. I regret running out on Wendy, and I called her to apologize for my rude behavior. I can't believe I did that!

I'm looking to buy a house in Valley Ranch, and I came close to finding the right one. I know it's out there and feel good about the area.

January 5, 2003 [Aware of Unforgiveness]

On Friday, Luke came over and then we went to see a movie. As we left my apartment, Marie was on her way out! I told

him how she used to be my friend and she started avoiding
me at a time when I needed her most. I wish I was healed; but
every time I see her, it strikes a chord in me.

January 12, 2003 [Burden of Unforgiveness]
Luke's birthday is today. We met for dinner, and I gave him a
framed reprint of the Jesus painting by Pastor Ed.

Home team's topic was about forgiveness. We each carried
a brick representing the heavy burden of unforgiveness. I still
carry a lot of hurt from Marie. It was fading until I saw her the
other night. **I must release it and need God's help! I can't
do it alone!** It's eating me up.

January 14, 2003 [Out of the Ashes]
You'll never guess what happened—I got an email from Jake
in Chicago! It was long, alluding to a family tragedy last
summer. He confessed to sneaking a peek at the last hardware
show, but didn't approach me. His band has been traveling
more since completing their fourth album. Jake said my song
[the one he wrote for me] turned out beautifully; I figured it
died when he broke things off.

Forgiveness has been at the forefront of my mind. I forgave
him last year (remember the card I sent?). Well, he never
received it! I prayed when I dropped it in the mailbox that God
would deliver it or it would get misrouted. Wow!

I wrote back telling Jake that I had forgiven him. We might
remain friends, but we can never have what we used to. **I'm
no longer the same Charlotte he remembers.** I will pray
for him again, as I know God is calling out to him. I sense he
is unsettled within his soul. I remember that feeling before I
discovered and accepted Jesus Christ.

January 28, 2003
Since being in Cleveland for sales training, I've had more time
to think about Luke. He's not right for me. Maybe I sensed it

earlier but waited until I knew in my gut. Now I have the grim
task of telling him.

Luke just called, but I let the machine pick up. I'm unsure
of what to say.

February 6, 2003

I terminated the contract on the Valley Ranch house on the
final day of the option period. Something wasn't right. I
woke up depressed and cried in the shower. I called Mom and
shared my concerns about the house, my job, and Luke. It was
a tough week.

I broke things off with Luke yesterday. I couldn't wait any
longer. I cried, not wanting to hurt him.

February 19, 2003 [First Ski Trip]

I'm in Colorado with Fellowship Church! Ski school was
great. I only fell once getting off the chair lift and once going
down a different way with small hills [moguls]. I picked up
speed, lost control, and laughed until I fell into a powdery
spot! No injuries! José, a guy on the trip, helped me up and
we skied down together. To my surprise, I was faster than the
other girls. I felt confident and in control.

I'm thankful Cheri [home team leader] is here, because
we've spent a lot of time together! Thank you, God, for
keeping me safe on this wild ski adventure!

February 22, 2003 [Speaking Truth]

I had a rough day at work and cried. I don't want to do
welding sales anymore. I'm also troubled because one of the
snooty girls on the ski trip is Pastor Fred's girlfriend! How can
someone God-centered like him choose someone like her? She
doesn't come across as a Christian at all.

I emailed Fred on Thursday, after rereading my message
several times. **I spoke the cold, hard truth, and now wonder
if I was too harsh.** He called Friday and left me a voice mail;

I returned his call on Saturday. I hope he calls back so we can be on the same page. I wonder if he shared my email with others at the church. Will they think I attacked Fred? Will they look down on me? Have I done anything wrong?

Renee is proud that I approached Fred, but she doesn't know the words I used: "Either you are fooling yourself by dating this girl, or you are fooling the rest of us that you are a true man of Christ." I refused to sugarcoat the truth—this is serious. Two female home team leaders also had run-ins with her. Who knows how many feel the same way?

Lord, I pray for Fred and his girlfriend. I also pray that we'll talk, put this behind us, and keep our eyes on you.

February 24, 2003 [Confessing and Praying]

I confessed my struggles at home team during prayer requests. **I realized for the first time that people at a church can range from inspiring Christians to seemingly non-Christians by the way they act.**

I prayed all weekend, numerous times. Fred hasn't called or emailed. I sent another email, because I don't want him to feel criticized or attacked. I quoted Romans 12:9: "Don't pretend to love others. Really love them. Hate what is wrong. Stand on the side of the good" (NLT). I hope this gives peace to Fred. As a new Christian, I'm concerned and confused.

March 6, 2003 [Answered Prayer]

I toured six homes in Lewisville and liked the first one immediately. The next day I submitted an offer. We close on April 15.

Thank you, Lord, for blessing me with this house!

March 10, 2003 [My Recurring Desire]

My manager and I spoke about my intentions. I don't want to work in the welding industry, period. It's not the city, the people, or the money; **I want to work somewhere I can**

use my God-given talents instead of forcing myself to be something I'm not. The economy is grim and many are unemployed. I fear not, because God will provide.

March 14, 2003

The house inspections went well—foundation, roof, furnace, and water heater are in good condition. Mom comes Easter weekend to help me move. My parents are helping with the down payment, leaving me with savings in the bank.

God continues to bless me in so many ways!

March 20, 2003 [First Volunteering Role]

I feel overwhelmed [with moving and other issues]. I started crying in the Thomasville Furniture store, and the sales lady asked if I was going through a divorce. Of course, I'm not even married, so I left the store in a bad mood.

I started packing this week and cleaning out drawers. I have 3 bags for the church clothing drive.

I completed my application and background check to volunteer at the church pre-school. It'll be about a week before I hear back.

March 28, 2003 [Sharing about Jesus]

I shared my faith with Jake (Chicago) over email. He's pretty much against all religions and is agnostic. He doesn't have a problem with me becoming a Christian; yet he probably doesn't know what it really means. I delicately shared my thoughts on the Bible and Jesus. I continue to pray for him as his heart is surely hardened. Jake is so anti-God, it's sad. Maybe he'll come around?

April 2, 2003 [Nudged by the Spirit]

Wow, First Wednesday was moving! Things stirred inside of me and I teared up several times. I am so humbled by the awesome power and wonder of God! **After the service, I saw**

Fred and felt I should introduce myself but didn't. I don't
know what to say. Shall I ask for forgiveness?

Lord, you will have to give me strength for this! Just when
I think it's behind me, it rises to the surface. What shall I learn
that I haven't already?

Work is more stressful with Texas Motor Speedway races,
Saturday sales call, my vacation next week, house closing, and
distributor training—all the while, selling machines for the
Power Drive promo, inviting customers to a seminar, updating
the end-user database, and more!

Lord, is there a job better suited for me?

April 10, 2003 [First Cruise]

I'm off on another journey—this time to Cozumel, Mexico,
on a cruise ship! I hope other young adults will be on board—
preferably, young men in their early thirties! How many single
guys go on a cruise?

God was good to me this past week! He helped me endure
my daily work challenges.

May 6, 2003 [First House]

Another month gone by! I closed on April 15. For 3 weeks,
Mom and I exhausted ourselves packing, loading, unloading,
cleaning, moving, painting, organizing, etc. I'm sick with
an upset stomach and threw up before driving Mom to the
airport.

The future is uncertain for me. My manager wants a
timeline of when I plan to leave. I don't think I can hang on
another six months.

Lord, let it be your will, not mine. I don't want to get in
the way. I feel disoriented and far removed from you. The past
month exhausted me, leaving me ill and uncertain. Refresh me
and recharge me, for I need your strength to make it through.

June 16, 2003 [Miracles in God's Timing]

I decided to stay with Lincoln until October. The national sales manager is coming to Dallas next week and wants to meet with every salesperson individually. I'll need to do some major praying!

I became the Saturday night contact for our home team. Cheri snuck it on me. I must be the most regular attendee.

A miracle happened at First Wednesday at Fellowship. After the service, I followed Cheri to get a T-shirt. On the way, I locked eyes with Fred, the singles pastor. I have prayed for weeks that God would put him in front of me! I realized that I must approach. I introduced myself and said, "I feel bad about some of the things I said [in my email] and wanted you to know that I'm sorry." He smiled and said, "Okay." Then Cheri returned and we left to get our shirts. He was very nice about it and I felt great! A load lifted off my mind and heart; I'm at peace with Fred. I called Renee, and she shared my joy! She had also prayed for resolution.

Not only that, but the Sunday service [a few days later] was about apologizing and humbling ourselves! We must ask for forgiveness with the intention of changing and learning from our mistakes. Did that ever fit with what transpired between Fred and me!

Thank you, God, for taking me through this. I've learned so much. I pray to never lose sight of your lessons and my mistakes.

June 24, 2003 [Break-in/My Baptism]

It's 1:30 a.m., and I haven't slept well at all. I had a stressful day that started with finding the demo van with a broken window and missing welding equipment! I was the last person to drive it. My manager is out of town, so I filed a police report.

Enough of the bad news. **The good news is, I was baptized at Fellowship Church!** Yeah! Lori from home team joined me. Amanda, Wendy, José, and others cheered us on. Marie sat in the crowd a few feet from the baptism line—I could not believe it! *Why* was she there? I was already nervous enough with the large crowd and Pastor Fred as the announcer. Lori and I were baptized at the same time. I'm glad I wasn't alone!

July 19, 2003

I find myself drawn to José, although he doesn't fit my image of a potential life companion. He has a great personality and contagious laugh. I pray to not rush into another relationship just because I find him attractive. I have to evaluate him as a person and potential spouse. God has someone great, don't you? I must be patient and obedient.

Thank you, Lord, for the blessings you give! Help me shine your light to others.

August 19, 2003 [Bro says No]

My brother, sister-in-law, and niece came to Dallas earlier this month. We enjoyed the park and pool, but I wasn't able to get them to church. I tried persuading and objection handling, but it didn't change the outcome.

My home team game night was at my house during Renee's visit. By the end of the night, there were twenty-three people in my living room! Wendy stayed after to talk about her unemployment; she is very scared, and Renee could relate. Before Wendy left, Renee and I prayed over her.

I took Renee to Fellowship on Saturday and showed her around. She was blown away! Ed continued his series, "Just Lust."

September 3, 2003

Okay, I'm pissed. It's been a while since I've been this way. **I confess my sins of jealousy and selfishness up front,**

because I am about to purge the contents of my brain on paper! It won't be pretty.

Last weekend was Labor Day. The weekend before, José and I went out after church. He called the next day, visited home team, and walked me to my car. We spoke again before I went to the lake. Today is Wednesday and he hasn't called. *No sweat,* I thought, *he'll see me tonight at church.* I spotted him across the room. By the time I reached that area, he was gone. *Strange,* I thought. *He usually waits for m*e.

A few minutes later, José walked up with a short blonde. Probably friends—fine. During our talk about wakeboarding, she said, "I've been trying to get this guy to learn how to wakeboard," and she swatted him playfully. He laughed and she laughed, while the voice in my head freaked out! I stood there with a fake smile, thinking, *Get me out of here!* It wasn't long before he said to me, "Well, we're going to take off," and I wanted to scream!

Apparently, I have feelings for him and wanted to move ahead slowly. Looks like I've been replaced. Why am I jealous? I told him last month that we should remain friends. Since then, we've met several times and he's called consistently. Part of me wants to call him, but is there anything to talk about?

Chris arrived last week. He's my replacement at Lincoln Electric [who will eventually receive my sales territory]. Can I hang on until bonus day on December 10? I posted my resume on Monster.com. So far, no phone calls.

September 22, 2003 [Mom Meets Church Friends]

My parents are in town and arrived 3 days ago. Work has been challenging, and I haven't slept well.

I've calmed down about the José issue. He left me a voice mail the following week. I called him back, since he didn't make it to church Saturday night. Mom came with me and met

my home team friends. Dad chose to stay home to work on my
deck railing.

September 26, 2003 [Peace Returns]

God came through for me—when José and I talked on the
phone, I felt no jealousy, sadness, or anger. We are friends. He
is dating that girl—my intuition was correct! As José shared
about her, I didn't feel envious; I was happy for him and
excited. I pray that I'll feel the same if I *see* them together.

November 3, 2003 [New Ministry]

Cheri approached me about volunteering in the singles
ministry's Single Impact, aka "SI: After the Service." One of
the pastors called and invited me to a leadership meeting. **I
felt the Lord lead me away from the preschool to get more
involved in Single Impact.**

Fallapalooza was last Friday and I helped with the
decorations and balloons. Our home team dressed up as the
Fellowship Church staff! Brett was Pastor Ed Young, Cheri
was Lisa Young . . . and I was Vanessa [church worship
singer]. We came in second place out of ten teams. I had so
much fun!

December 21, 2003 [Blessings and Warfare]

Hard to believe 2003 is almost history! There were many
blessings: ski trip, cruise to Mexico, my first house, parents'
3-week visit, my baptism, hosting home team, tithing the full
10 percent, volunteering at preschool and Single Impact, and
learning more about God, Christ, and myself!

**I have experienced spiritual warfare this year for the
first time.** Every step I took toward God and His will, the
more the devil plagued my thoughts and messed with my
head. He used guys as a distraction, feeding me lies and wild
stories, even in my dreams!

The Christmas series started at Fellowship. I felt the Holy Spirit rise up, and I cried during "O Night Divine"—tears of joy and gratitude for all that God has done in my life. It's overwhelming!

I'm almost done with *The Purpose Driven Life*.

My job search is slow and unfruitful. God is having me wait—for how long and for what, I don't know.

I sent Marie a Christmas card this year, wishing her well. [We hadn't communicated since running into each other the night of my baptism.] She called me at the office and we played phone tag. Finally, we connected and talked for an hour! It was awkward, but for the best. God has returned her into my life for a reason, and I cannot deny it. We met for a two-hour lunch, but I felt a gap between us, or a resistance to open up. I can't tell if she has changed.

I need to nurture more friendships in 2004. **I want to spend more time with the Lord in prayer and in the Bible.** This has been on my heart for months.

January 10, 2004 [On Stage]

Wow, I've attended Fellowship Church for almost two years. That's about the time I started disliking my job, but I'm still here!

Something funny (out of the norm) happened at Single Impact. One of the pastors asked if he could call me on stage to answer questions about the ski retreat in order to advertise for the upcoming trip. I said, "Sure. (Pause) I kind of have stage fright, but I'll do it." And I did. Overall, it went well, although I did reach for the mic when he leaned it closer to me to answer the first question. Reflexes I guess, and I had never been around microphones because they make me nervous!

January 30, 2004 [Prayer of Influence]

I applied for another job at Fellowship 3 weeks ago, and they have already picked their candidate. Otherwise, the job search

has been very unfruitful. I figure this means that the Lord
wants me to focus on other things, like spending time with
Him in the Word and in prayer. I still haven't gotten up early
for quiet time.

A girl at the gym approached me and said she had visited
my home team back in November. She has been a Christian
for 3 years (me, one and a half years) and is so on fire for the
Lord! A Beth Moore Bible study changed her life—"Breaking
Free?"

I saw a blonde girl I recognized at church. She's the single
saleswoman I met on the airplane over Christmas! Isn't that
amazing? We exchanged business cards, but neither one of us
has called the other.

I finished the book *The Prayer of Jabez*. **It's supposed to
be the most powerful prayer that one can pray to totally
change and enhance their walk with the Lord!** I need to
pray it every day.

February 14, 2004

Valentine's Day! I slept late and awoke to children laughing
and playing in the snow. Yes, I said snow! Dallas got 3 inches
last night!

Tomorrow I fly to Houston for 3 days of training with
my Dallas coworkers. In two weeks, I'll be in Michigan for
robotics training. Last weekend I flew to San Antonio for
some family time.

Thank you, Lord, for all that you do for me and for
accepting me the way I am.

March 7, 2004

Our national sales manager (my boss's boss) invited me to
participate in a crisis-management team in Cleveland for 3
months [assisting with the welding wire shortage]. I'm excited
to break from life in Dallas. My job has weighed on my heart

and emotions the past few months, and more than ever, I want out.

Today, I might be depressed. Even with church and home team activities, they smother me at times. I took on a leadership role at Single Impact, and I've hosted home team for five months. I wonder how it affects me, since I usually don't sleep well afterwards.

I told a friend that I feel overwhelmed. I also feel lonely. More and more friends are getting married and having kids. My roommate from my 1997 summer internship had a baby boy, as did Amy from Lincoln's training class. Another home team leader is engaged, and the list could go on but I'll stop. Nisa and I are still single, and so is Renee.

In lieu of my "job depression," I wish I didn't have to work anymore! That would simplify my life. **I feel so far from where I need to be, from where God wants me.** Am I not doing the right things that He wants? Is Fellowship the best church to meet my needs? Is it supposed to be about me? Others' needs are more important.

June 9, 2004

Well, it's been almost 3 months since my last journal entry. I'm at the Residence Inn in Beachwood, Ohio, and another thunderstorm has rolled through. It has rained more and been overcast twice as much as it has been sunny. [I've been working at Lincoln Electric's headquarters allocating welding wire shipments with two other ladies.]

June 20, 2004

Well, it's past my bedtime but I can't sleep. Perhaps it's the wine or the fact that I'm leaving in less than 3 days. I'm going back to Dallas at last! ☺

On Friday, I leave for Sanibel Island, Florida. I need a vacation! And a massage!

July 31, 2004 [My Debt Paid]

I've been back in Big D four weeks now. I don't have a
volunteer position at Single Impact yet. One of the leaders
invited me to be his co-chair over all 3 singles classes, but I
don't think I will accept.

Renee came two weeks ago for a 3-day visit. We split the
pancake short stack at Jackie's Ham 'n Eggs. **I forgot they
only take cash or check—no VISA—but a God thing
happened.** [Distressed, I had told Renee that] I lacked cash
to pay our bill, and the lady behind me handed me $7! It
was Pastor Ed's wife, Lisa! I thanked her and wished her a
wonderful day. I didn't call her out. She was doing a good
deed because God stirred her heart, and I didn't want to shine
a spotlight on her. What a neat miracle!

I had my first Power Source class about studying the Bible
and getting more from reading the Word. I tend to miss the
true meaning and want help!

Texas Woman's University in Denton offers a Masters in
the Art of Teaching (MAT). I could be done in one year if I go
full-time.

August 7, 2004

I can't fall asleep. My parents arrived last night, and my
brother's family arrived at 2:00 a.m. today. We talked until
3:30 a.m. then returned to bed. I feel sad and distant, perhaps
frustrated with the commotion. What's my problem? Too much
noise, not enough relax time? This is the 3rd night that I've
slept poorly. Is it spiritual warfare? **As I draw closer to God
through daily Bible time, home team studies, and church
services, I feel something robbing my joy and peace.**

I felt better after church (my family went to Olive Garden),
but at my home team's cookout, I felt blah. It was hard to
smile and socialize. After an hour, I left feeling like I may cry.
My whole day was frustrating. I drove home asking God to
help me, fix me, and restore my joy and peace. Pastor Tracy

spoke tonight about worshipping 24/7. Is this God's way of testing me?

September 14, 2004

I registered for the qualifying exam for TWU's MAT program. I'm thinking about teaching high school chemistry. Teaching allows me to be creative and prepare teens for college. What an inspiration my chemistry teacher was to me at Troy High School! Do I have the God-given gift to become an extraordinary teacher? Am I patient enough?

Dear Lord, please bless me! Bless me with discernment for my planned career change. **Excited and scared, I move ahead with the preparation. Please guide me if I go off course.** Bring me my Christian husband, so strong and faithful! May I learn to die to myself—I no longer live, but Christ lives in me (Galatians 2:20). Amen!

November 24, 2004

I'm at DFW airport waiting to fly to Michigan for Thanksgiving. What a year, although it's not over! Big moments:

- Went to Cleveland for 3½ months to allocate welding wire shipments
- Hired Dianna [yoga instructor] as my personal trainer and developed a friendship
- Met Marie for lunch
- Steff had her first baby [answered prayer from 2002]
- Turned twenty-eight years old
- Hosted home team for one year
- Shared my faith with my boss on the drive back from Wichita Falls
- Grew closer to Wendy
- Paid off the Maxima!

November 25, 2004

I made it to Detroit safely after unexpected turbulence. Despite my window seat, I felt confined and cramped. My knees were one-eighth inch from the seat ahead, and there were 3 of us in the row. The guy in front of me reclined all the way, decreasing my breathing space! This was my first time feeling sick on a plane.

My ten-year Troy High School reunion is tomorrow! Nisa's bringing her new boyfriend. Amy's sister will be there with her fiancé. She teaches elementary school, so we must talk!

I'm waiting for my transcripts to complete the graduate school application. I plan to leave Lincoln mid-January and submit my resignation letter in December. I'm taking a leap of faith, no matter what society will say!

God, help me stay strong to execute your will for my life! Glory to God—not to us, but to your name!

December 10, 2004 [Trusting God]

Bonus day! I was rewarded extra points for going to Cleveland. This translates to about $3,300 more income than last year.

My transcripts arrived, and my TWU application is now in process. It may be weeks before I get a letter in the mail, but I've done everything I can to push it through or speed it up. **Now it's in God's hands to control the university's action and the final outcome.**

December 13, 2004

I shared my preresignation news with Wendy and she was shocked. Two days until I drop the news on my manager. I wrote a rough draft and pray for peace beyond understanding.

Give me strength and courage, dear Lord! I will follow!

December 18, 2004 [My First Resignation]

I handed my manager the letter 3 days ago. My stomach was in knots and I felt tired and weak. But after it was out in the open, I felt better!

I don't feel that most people understand why I want to be a teacher. Why give up a high-paying sales job? Why live off your savings [to go back to college]? **I pray for the ability to disregard their concerns and listen only to God's voice of direction.**

I'm still waiting for my acceptance letter from TWU.

January 1, 2005 [Church with Sister-in-law]

Happy New Year! Christmas was in San Antonio. My sister-in-law, Mom, and I visited Oak Hills Church, where author Max Lucado is pastor. I'm glad my sister-in-law took us but sad that she didn't like the music, building, or contemporary style. She grew up Catholic. Hopefully God planted a seed in her heart.

Let 2005 be a year to release my *fears* and step out in *faith*!

January 4, 2005

One week remaining at Lincoln Electric. All the stress, expectations, and pressures from the past six and a half years are vaporized! My spirit feels cleansed and renewed. After years of mental suffering and walking through the desert of isolation, God has brought me through. My next season begins.

It's been two years since I have been on a date, but I was asked out at the New Year's party! Too bad I'm not interested.

January 9, 2005 [Answered Prayer]

I received my official acceptance letter from TWU's Graduate School on Friday the 7th!!! Now I meet my advisor and register for classes. I'm very happy, as I know it is

God's will! The doors have stayed open every step of the way since the MAT seminar in July.

January 13, 2005

Yesterday was my last day at Lincoln Electric! I stayed late, finishing expenses and packing belongings. I visited [my favorite customers] to say goodbye and almost cried.

Today I went to TWU and I met my advisor. The 3 EDUC classes are offered through the internet, so I'll use my new home computer. I have no remorse leaving Lincoln. What an amazing experience to change careers and walk through the fear to get to the other side!

January 20, 2005 [Miracle/Academic Seas Part]

I dropped READ 5423 today. The class felt unnatural, making me wonder if elementary is a good fit. If I teach science, I can choose grades 4-8 or 8-12, but they aren't listed in the MAT program. The last day to add/drop classes is tomorrow.

Bonnie [TWU staff member] dropped my READ class and added Earth Science. I had walked all over campus getting signatures and then returned to the Registrar's Office to finalize my schedule and pay the late fee. I went to the bookstore, bought the *last* two books, and then attended my two-hour orientation. Whew!

I'm specializing in 4-8 Science, which exists on a case-by-case basis. It was a miracle by God's grace that while I was in Bonnie's office, a student in another building dropped Earth Science! Bonnie left a voice mail to save that spot; the class was full and had been for a while. Vicky had a waiting list of students, but she gave that spot to *me*! Praise God! I almost cried!

God is leading me every step of the way and has made the impossible happen for me to get my classes. Literally—by one cancellation—I've slid into *3 classes* this semester!

Thank you, God, for your direction and open doors at TWU. I'm in awe!

February 7, 2005

[I'm having doubts about teaching middle school.] I have to decide to certify in 4-8 Science or 8-12 Chem/Physics. If I teach high school, how difficult are the concepts and how comfortable will I feel teaching them? It's been almost 7 years since I studied chemistry.

February 13, 2005 [Sabbath Rest]

I had a fun day! I got up early, cleaned house, and spent quiet time with the Lord. Wendy and I had lunch in Fort Worth, and then we walked to Bass Performance Hall for the ballet *Five of Hearts*.

Home team ended after 9:00 p.m. It is 10:20 p.m., and I'm wide awake. Is it the coffee? **Maybe it's just the excitement of seeing God work in my life.** I'm learning to let go and watch Him take care of things.

Pastor Ed talked about working six days with one day of rest, per God's decree. Today was my day of rest. I did clean for an hour, but the rest of the day was fun, fun, fun!

February 27, 2005

Yesterday was my rest day. After yoga, Wendy and I watched *The Aviator*. It won an Oscar for Best Picture and 3 or four other categories.

Our home team leaders are engaged! Another couple, too! I continue to be dateless; but since New Year's Eve, I have been asked out by four guys. That's more than all of last year!

March 28, 2005

Mom's visit was very productive and enjoyable. We had a great conversation about my future as a teacher, my past with Lincoln, and my challenges at the University of Michigan. I told her about the TExES [teacher certification test] and how I must pass the chemistry and physics sections because the classes required for my degree are determined by my test scores.

I studied physics for eight hours on Wednesday. I have two more days to prepare.

Dad finished the deck at my brother's house. Absolutely amazing! He's 77 years old!

April 12, 2005 [Divine Appointments]

The TExES (Physical Science) was tough. It took five hours to answer ninety questions.

The National Science Teachers Association Convention was in Dallas. I met Robert, an Oklahoma high school teacher, while waiting for the shuttle. We walked around and ate lunch together. I asked about teaching and shared some of my fears. It was fun to have someone to talk to, especially an experienced teacher.

A God-thing happened several times that day: (1) I met Jane from Arkansas, who told me about Flinn Scientific workshops; (2) at their booth, I learned they will be in Denton this June; (3) I met Robert after saying goodbye to Jane; and (4) after lunch, I felt a strong urge for a piece of gum. When I rejoined Robert, he had a pack of gum in his hand and said, "Want a piece?" I was thrilled! Something so little, and yet I *knew* it was God!

I'm getting reconnected with Single Impact, coordinating check-in volunteers.

I finished the eight-week class "Dollars & Sense." It was insightful, opening my eyes to God's view of money and how much I'm spending. I estimated a budget based on a teacher's salary. It'll be tight with my expenses and tithing.

May 21, 2005 [Answered Prayers]

My yoga instructor saw a sign—"Secretary needed"—on her drive home. I called them seeking a part-time summer job. They had already found a secretary but may need help organizing and filing. I dropped off my resume with the president. He offered a flexible schedule, working as much as I want. It's perfect! I accepted the job after scheduling my classes—all 3 are online. **Amazing how God brought this together!**

My scores from the TExES 8-12 Physical Science exam arrived. I passed! ☺

Other news: I found out that I have scoliosis—a 30-degree curvature in my lower back. I had a free spinal evaluation with X-rays at a local chiropractor. The scoliosis developed because my left leg is one-half inch shorter than my right. Also, I found out that my neck is straight up and down instead of having a C-curve. This means that my head sits too far forward on my neck, which causes tension and knots in my lower neck and shoulders. I may need chiropractic treatment or physical therapy; I must do more research.

May 27, 2005

Here I sit at DFW airport, Terminal C, waiting for my flight to Raleigh to visit Renee. I got my first paycheck from my summer employer yesterday. It's a nice feeling to put money in the bank again.

June 2, 2005

Back in Big D after a wonderful time with Renee. We watched *What Not to Wear* and played sand volleyball with her friends. Yes, I played, although I didn't want to. My first serve in fourteen years was perfect, but what followed was a disaster! I can't say that I enjoyed it because I was nervous and uncomfortable. Everyone there was very good.

June 26, 2005 [Spiritual Warfare/Mental Attacks]

Classes started with a *bang*! I'm drowning in a sea of assignments while juggling twenty hours of work and 3 workouts per week, volunteering Saturdays, and hosting home team twice a month. It's funny—people ask me to lead our home team, but I don't have the mental capacity. I already feel overwhelmed with my current duties.

I struggle to remain grounded when issues arise at Single Impact. Last night, I tried keeping everything running smoothly. People wanted to chitchat, but my mind couldn't focus on them; it was focused on the current computer problem [that prevented us from printing name tags for the singles arriving at the event]! **I have a hard time switching gears and feel anxious until the issues are resolved.** Before the speaker began, I already felt disappointed and discouraged by how I handled things. My peace was gone. I wanted to join the group, but issues arose that prevented me from finishing [my volunteer duties]. Then a *roar* of laughter came from the main room, and instantly I felt sad to be missing out again. I came home frustrated, sad, and confused at my emotions. My period starts in 3 days, if that explains anything. I felt useless during event set-up and clean-up. I didn't sleep well and woke up twice. I thought journaling may clear my head.

Sometimes I feel like I have a mental illness. Voices talking back and forth in my head saying: "You should do this" or "Don't do that." "Why aren't you helping?" "They're waiting on you." "You aren't fast enough." "What's your problem?" It's like a jumbled bunch of signals shooting around in my brain. They distract me from my duties at Single Impact. **Maybe I'm not mentally unstable, but am experiencing the attacks of Satan.** I should pray harder before volunteering to limit the interference.

August 21, 2005

I finished classes with another 4.0 and passed the qualifying teaching exam!

My sister-in-law is twelve weeks pregnant. She's thirty-six and is worried about birth defects. **I pray that God protects the baby and keeps it healthy through term and beyond.**

Our S-10 Home Team is no more—3 couples got married, and no one wanted to lead.

August 27, 2005 [First Christian Conference]

Friday was my last day at my summer job. I felt certain the Lord placed me there to act as a reflection of His love, and I tried my best to be an example. The secretary and I went out for lunch, and I invited her to church. She's twenty-four with two kids and separated from her husband.

The Women of Faith Conference was amazing! My eyes were swollen from crying, but there was laughter too. Key points: God is in control; He forgives *and* forgets; tragedy strikes all of us—it's not punishment; God's timing is perfect; we are to spread the love of Christ with everyone; we don't argue others into accepting Christ; life doesn't follow our plan; and things don't turn out the way we envisioned, but God is faithful.

I pray to apply the principles and truths from the conference. I was greatly impacted and don't want to return to my old self! Jesus did *not* come so that I would be a slave to the thinking of this world, but to set me *free* and give me joy, peace, and comfort. There's no need to fear when you have faith in the Lord Almighty!

September 25, 2005

I started my final semester at TWU. **I thought I was going to take the lab as a student, but God had another plan.** I was offered the opportunity of assisting the teacher's assistant for general chemistry. She and I have instructed 3 labs so far.

This will sound girlish and silly, but I met a guy tonight.
They come so few and far between—guys that I want to get
to know. Paul participated in the home team discussion and
seems committed in his faith.

Lord, don't let this go to my head, where I daydream a
fairytale romance!

September 30, 2005

Mom was rear-ended driving home in the station wagon.
Thank the Lord, she's all right! She was supposed to come
for two weeks, but she's in a splint with crutches. My heart is
heavy, since we planned to celebrate my birthday together.

I pray the Lord will surround me with friends on my
birthday. I don't want to be alone! I guess I'm lonely, locked
up for days doing classwork.

Father, please heal my mom and her spirit, if it's wounded
like mine. We will be together again.

November 2, 2005

Mom is healing well and begins physical therapy this week.
She didn't need a cast (great news) and the splint is history.
It'll be a while before she drives again.

I taught the pre-lab lecture on thermochemistry. It went
very well!

Paul, the new visitor from September, has surfaced again—
he was at First Wednesday. I forgot how attractive he is!
Trying to ignore that, I had a few words with him as we left
the worship center.

Lord, I'm giving you everything to take care of—thoughts,
hopes, dreams, and worries. I refuse to live in a fantasy world.
Keep me grounded if and when I talk to Paul again.

December 17, 2005 [Public Meltdown]

Not my best day. Not my proudest moment. **I had a
meltdown at the single's Winter Wonderland!** My stress

threshold was surpassed. The White Elephant gift exchange had nobody to lead it, so the singles coordinator told me to run it! I did *not* have the mental capacity to do so but tried anyway. I lacked the patience needed to shout over the karaoke. The coffee station went down when a circuit blew, and someone called the security guard. Meanwhile, greeters asked me questions and pointed out details that were overlooked.

I almost started crying 3 or four times. I felt blindsided and ill-prepared. I tried doing too much because we didn't have enough volunteers. I talked with a staff member in the back office. I was crying and so embarrassed. People in the main room—I don't know how many—saw me lose it. I felt like I had let my team down for being weak and inferior. A friend grabbed my coat and purse, and I left [while the event was in progress]. My head replays the events over and over. I'm trying to let go.

Help me, Jesus, to release my anxieties. You know I did my best despite the circumstances. Help me to know that you love me and that others' thoughts are irrelevant. Let me surrender all to you!

December 28, 2005

I should be sleeping—too much on my mind. I landed a paid internship at a local high school! Instead of student teaching, I'll earn a full teacher salary. [Answered prayer! I *really* wanted to teach at this particular school.]

Paul's in Peru sending long emails (like Jake used to). I'm "sucked in," addicted to receiving his next message. I spent an hour emailing the past two nights and haven't slept well. I wonder if God's trying to get my attention.

January 14, 2006 [Blessing Is a Curse]

My internship started January 3. I arrived at 8:00 a.m. and stayed until 9:30 p.m. on the teacher workday. The following

3 days, I arrived at 7:30 a.m. and stayed until 7:30 p.m. and *still* wasn't ready for the next lesson! I worked two hours at home, went to bed, rolled around, and got up before 3:00 a.m. to finish preparing. It was indescribable.

My appetite was nothing the first 3 days of school. I asked teachers for help, but not soon enough. **I thought with more time and effort, I could figure it out.** I was wrong. When grading started, I had more than I could handle! I phoned in absent Tuesday and quit by two o'clock. I didn't feel better, although you would think I would've. I was disappointed in how I handled things. I didn't know how to ask for help.

Now, I'm waiting on my placement for student teaching. I pray the Lord places me with a fabulous teacher.

January 20, 2006

My placement is at a different high school, starting on the 23rd. I pray the teacher is a great role model and experienced with student teachers. I may be asking for a lot, but Charlotte's known to be picky!

We need rain! My house foundation is cracking due to shifting soil. I've run soaker hoses 3 days in a row for twenty to thirty minutes. My savings are shrinking fast. I'm praying about my foundation and my finances.

Paul is due home in February. We shared some personal stories, and I told him things no one else knows. Maybe that's the danger of email—you feel comfortable spilling your guts on a screen and you take a chance of saying too much.

I'm struggling with my thoughts. I daydream of how things could be, and in my head, I know a guy more than in reality. I wish I could turn it off. I don't want to get hurt because of my own doing. It'll be 3 years since my last date/relationship.

February 1, 2006 [Angry at God]
I attended First Wednesday with a hard heart. There was
no emotion in my singing. I'm angry at God because He let
me fail at [the teaching internship]. I'm angry that my savings
will deplete to zero dollars in the next few months. I'm angry
that He has led me into a career that will take *more* of my time
than when I was in sales! I tried to avoid becoming a slave to
my job, and yet the chains are clamping down. I'm jealous of
the stay-at-home moms who are living my dream! I want to be
married.

February 10, 2006 [First Day Student Teaching]
Yesterday I taught my first class as a student teacher. I
used an electronic tablet, which locked up—low battery!
An unplanned fire drill (i.e., bomb threat) during 3ʳᵈ period
shortened fourth period, and my topic was electron
configuration—not the easiest concept to explain. Lord knows,
I did my best!
     Today was tough. My mentor teacher Edward made a rude
comment. I was speechless! It hurt my feelings, because I
really tried to get involved but didn't understand the lab. Later,
I graded papers while he babbled headlines; I didn't look up.
For the first time, he waited to walk to lunch. Without looking
at him, I said, "I'll catch up later." **I needed time to pray; I
was teaching after lunch, and I was pissed.**
     The science teachers sat in a circle eating Chick-fil-A, and
I really wanted to be alone. My food was cold and the melted
cheese wouldn't scrape off! My frustration increased, but I
tried looking happier than I felt. I asked about the brownies—
gone! So I paid five dollars for a four-dollar meal and got
gypped out of a brownie. I just wanted to leave!
     Praise God, I sucked it up, put on a happy face, and made it
through fourth period! I made several mistakes but was elated
to be done! But when Edward talked to me afterwards, my
spirits sank again. Perhaps I needed him to praise some part of

my lesson, but he didn't. Is he capable of meeting my needs as a student teacher? Am I too needy? I know I'm too sensitive. I almost lost it at lunchtime—so close to tears!

March 5, 2006

God granted my request for peace with student teaching! I taught five times, and my anxiety dropped. For the first time, I stood back and let God take over—it felt amazing!

Things with Edward improved. He still says and does things that irk me, but I expect it. He has many great qualities, but I see his flaws just as clearly. He's selfish and arrogant, but also sweet and funny. Sometimes he's flirty, but other times he's rude. I invited him to church as a general invitation. Only God knows if he'll go. Part of me is attracted to him, while the other part knows he's not a man of God. I pray for his soul and our friendship.

May you, Lord, change his heart to seek you! May you change *my* heart to be more compassionate and less bossy. I may have hurt his feelings when I said he was like the Tin Man from the Wizard of Oz—he needed a heart. Who am I to judge? I have just as many flaws that are probably obvious to others.

Paul and I went to a movie last week. He called tonight to say he's moving to Florida. He claims to hate it here. I thought he liked me and that may be enough reason to stay. Obviously not! But God is good, because I feel at peace.

March 25, 2006 [Satan Tempts]

I pray for self-control! I pray to shut off my active imagination and focus on other things—taxes, errands, groceries, etc. Edward is not a man of God, so why isn't that enough to dissipate the attraction? **Is lust fooling me to think a relationship may work?** Am I thinking of my own selfish needs and desires? Maybe both—*help*!

March 30, 2006 [Taking a Bite]

After home team, I spent 3 hours with Edward. We met for dinner and watched *Tommy Boy* at his apartment. (It's been over 3 years since I kissed a guy!)

I'll invite him to Fellowship for Easter. I'm praying for his salvation. I don't know the condition of his heart but sense he's far from God. I cannot change him; only Jesus can. **I may be foolish for pursuing a relationship that is not based upon Christ.** I pray for protection of my heart and mind.

April 16, 2006 [Spirit Convicts]

Edward joined me for church yesterday. I think he liked the service more than the music. Am I compromising my values and beliefs [by dating him]?

Only 3 weeks of student teaching remain. Will we still be dating?

I feel so confused right now. Is it spiritual warfare?

May 6, 2006 [Eyes Are Opened]

I'm very disappointed. Yesterday was my last day student teaching. Second and 3rd periods went well, but fourth was terrible. I wanted to leave in the middle of lecture.

Moreover, I'm disappointed with Edward. I saw an issue of *Maxim* magazine in his bathroom, and my heart sank. The cover had titles about sex, and I was horrified by an ad for CK cologne. It was a 3-page foldout with a blonde in a bikini crawling on the beach. It made me sick. I confronted him and he replied, "*Maxim* is no worse than *Sports Illustrated* swim suit edition." *Okay???* I asked if he also subscribed to that—he said no. He equated *Maxim* as being the "*Cosmo* for women." I told him that I don't read *Cosmo*.

I was hurt to realize that Edward was [indifferent to my concern]. Worse yet, he subscribed to *Maxim* through a student raising money to go to Africa! It's trash—filthy and dirty. I must end our relationship; and that means no prom next weekend, and I go back to struggling in life alone. **I'm paying the consequence for pursuing something that dishonors God.**

May 20, 2006 [Deceived and Disobedient]

I went to prom with Edward. He picked me up with a dozen red roses!

We're still dating. I'm trying to take God's lead, but I'm not sensing it. Whenever I prepare to break things off, something changes and I feel better. **I don't want to marry an unbeliever, but why don't I feel the push to let go?** All I can figure is that God wants me to wait. Bring him to church a few more times? I enjoy being with him.

I pray the Lord keeps me close and leads me in the proper direction. If I have strayed, please return me.

Another area needing direction is my church home. For the past few months, I sense discontent. I thought my heart was hardening, but tonight I feel God may be leading me to a new church? Things don't feel right, and they haven't since January. I thought I was battling disappointment, but maybe it's God's way of prompting me to look elsewhere?

May 23, 2006 [Sin Causes Pain]

A migraine headache started around 3:00 a.m. with thoughts of Edward churning in my head. I must end things. Even though I care for him, it won't work. I knew this from the start—he's not a Christ follower—and threw my better judgment aside. **I have always preached that I would never date a nonbeliever; it was insane.** Now I have proven my statement true. There's too much heartache.

May 30, 2006 [Return to Jesus]

Today I did it, crying before the words came out. He sat quietly and replied, "If that's how you feel, then we shouldn't force it to work." I guess I expected some sadness (like the last two guys I broke up with). Ironically, I pulled the plug, but I was the one crying! It shows how tightly I held on. I grieve losing the closeness, laughs, and fun times. He's a sweet guy with a big heart, but his roots are in the world, not Christ.

I thank the Lord for giving me courage to let go. I ask for healing for both of us.

May 31, 2006 [Healing Tears]

Isn't it funny how the morning after a breakup feels extra quiet? I prayed for restful sleep, but woke up many times. I prayed for a new day to walk closer to the Lord.

Last night, I cried while listening to my Shawn MacDonald CD. **At first, my tears were from letting go of something I wanted—companionship. By the end of the night, my tears were of remorse and healing.** I cried out to Jesus that I need Him. I strayed, but I need Him now more than ever. He will heal my wounds and bind up the brokenhearted.

I am still unemployed [and praying for a summer job and a permanent teaching job]. This is week four, and I'm getting restless.

I release all my fears, worries, and concerns to you, Lord, one day at a time.

[ALMOST ONE YEAR LATER...]

April 28, 2007

A quick recap of the past year:

- Worked one week at JC Penney print shop. [The supervisor noticed my work ethic and said there was something different about me—he asked if I was a Christian!]

- Received a call from my Lincoln manager about filling in for the Inside Sales lady who quit. [Answered prayer for a summer job!]

- Interviewed with Richardson ISD but lacked peace about the position. From there, I drove to Smith High School in Plano after receiving a call days earlier about an opening.

- Arrived at Smith, but the doors were locked! Discouraged, I went to my car and called my parents. I didn't have an interview, but I wanted this job. I found their phone number on my MapQuest printout. I called the office, was buzzed in, met the assistant principal, and was told to return in forty-five minutes. I returned to meet the principal, whom I liked immediately. I had peace, and she hired me on the spot! I joined the new-teacher orientation upstairs, saw my classroom, and got keys and a textbook!!! **It was a God-ordained miracle!** I went from the verge of driving home in defeat to getting *hired* and *starting* right away! [Answered prayer for a teaching job!]

- It's been a nine-month journey of learning to teach, making mistakes, discovering my style, and connecting with students. My biggest discipline challenges are with boys being rough, rude, or disrespectful. At first I was scared and nervous. I lived every moment clinging to Jesus for His strength and guidance.

- I haven't dated anyone in the last year.

- My second niece is one year old and walking. [Answered prayer from 2005 for a healthy baby!]

May 13, 2007

Today should be a beautiful Mother's Day after 3 weeks of rain and storms. My roof lost six to ten shingles, and water leaked into my master bedroom wall! Praise God, my neighbor Dana knew who to call for repair.

May 28, 2007 [Seed of Possibility]

Fellowship Church had a singles volleyball tournament. Scott was there, the tall guy I have my eye on. Two days ago at church, he walked by and we locked eyes for 3 seconds. That moment planted a seed in my mind that he may be interested. I don't want to overthink things, but I usually do! At the volleyball courts, Scott passed by looking at me. He caught me off guard. I froze, gave a quick smile, and turned around to get napkins! I looked up and he was gone. I wanted him to say "hi." Maybe I should've, but I was afraid.

I pray to focus my thoughts on God and release everything else into His hands. I'm *not* in control of my life.

June 9, 2007

Well, Father, I'm disappointed, insecure, and a bit confused. I don't want to replay the events anymore, because I'm probably overreacting. I just want to give it over to you.

Today at church, Christie [ski trip] was telling a mutual friend how God brought us together in the women's Bible study. (I agreed to host but needed a leader. She was scheduled to lead, but the host home fell through.) Scott was standing ten feet away, looking in our direction but *not* at me. My heart was hopeful we'd say hello until Christie walked over, touched his arm, and stood with his group. My stomach hit the floor! In that moment, which may have amounted to nothing more than jealousy, I felt invisible.

Does this mean Scott isn't interested in me? Is Christie
interested in Scott? A wave of insecurities rose up. Why am
I protective of guys I like? He's never asked me out. Did I
misinterpret his gazes?

I will never figure things out by thinking about them. I
release this to you, Lord!

August 5, 2007

The past two months were fantastic! After returning from
San Antonio, the women's summer Bible study started at my
house. We are reading *Having a Mary Spirit*. **I'm discovering
my fears, flaws, false beliefs, and who my "flesh woman"
is.** I led the study when Christie was out of town. I really
enjoyed chapter eight, and learned a lot from teaching it.

I haven't seen Scott in a month. Christie knows him from
an old home team, and said she'd be happy to introduce us.
That was June; it's August, and I'm doubtful.

August 20, 2007

Today was my first day back for teacher in-service. I got
up at 5:45 a.m., left at 7:15 a.m., and returned home with a
headache at 6:45 p.m. I plan to work late each night.

God has given me peace the past two months as I prepared
for my second year. **I can feel friends praying for me!** I
watched Joel Osteen's message, "Let God Be God." It's
a great reminder to keep my eyes on God, no matter what
challenges are ahead.

I met a guy, James, at single's class. We talked at our table
for fifteen minutes while people cleaned up around us. I
accepted his dinner invitation, although it was 10:00 p.m. and
my feet hurt from walking the scavenger hunt in heels!

Lord, I place this new friendship in your hands. I'm
interested in knowing James, and yet I wonder about Scott.
Only you know what will transpire. Please don't let me get
disappointed if things don't turn out the way I want. Thank

you for my joy, peace, and confidence. I felt gorgeous tonight
because of your love and my kicking outfit! ☺

September 8, 2007

James and I have exchanged 3 or four emails. He hasn't
invited me to do anything. Tonight was my first time seeing
him after the service, but I couldn't catch his eye. Earlier I saw
Scott but didn't catch his eye either.

Lord, I'm wrestling in my soul. As much as I want James
to ask me out, I want to capture Scott's heart. What I want and
what you want may be different; I lay down my selfish desires
and accept your will. I haven't waited for your advice on what
to do, if anything. I must seek *you* first, and all else will be
given unto me. Thank you for changing me!

September 15, 2007

Thank you for a fun time at church with the kindergarteners.
A church staff member is praying for strength, confidence, and
peace with my teaching and for a quiet heart regarding Scott.
I confessed that I pray about meeting him, and yet I also make
plans to get it done myself.

I didn't see James tonight, but I did see Scott. Our home
teams merged as we were leaving the worship center, and
Scott ended up next to me! My brain went blank. I missed
another chance, but will give this to the Lord. Only He knows
what He has for me. I don't want to think about it anymore!

Meanwhile, James emailed about hitting golf balls
sometime. This shows promise, but no date was set. I should
follow up with him before pursuing Scott (which I should *stop*
doing altogether).

September 24, 2007 [First Date]

James and I met at Starbucks. He has two sons and has
attended Fellowship for 3 years. Overall, I had a fun time and
so did he.

After our date, my car started strangely with the "service engine" light on. Today, it's dead. It has 127,000 miles and is only 7 years old. As I write, I'm waiting on a tow truck.

October 7, 2007 [Second Date]

I had an enjoyable day playing tennis with James. We sat outside at Chipotle talking for 3 hours! He is a member of Fellowship Church and has been baptized.

God's working on me, and I sense a small breakthrough. I can't explain it. My mind is more at peace with James and Scott. I released control back to God. When I'm with James, it feels so natural, like I can say anything and he won't reject me.

October 17, 2007 [Doubts]

Well, I'm feeling better after two days of food poisoning. Unfortunately, this extra time has birthed doubts about James's interest. It's been over a week since I last heard from him.

Today, I wrestled with my flesh about waiting for James to contact me. I broke down and sent him an email. **I must recognize Satan's role in all of this.** He's whispering doubts that I may have said something to scare James away, or maybe he's dating other women. I didn't have these thoughts until Tuesday, when there was no email from James.

Dr. Phil's book *Love Smart* says to not take it personally if a guy isn't thinking about me as often as I think about him. Men's minds are linear, focusing on one thing at a time. In James's case, this could be (a) work, (b) kids, or (c) ex-wife and divorce.

October 28, 2007 [Attacks Continue]

I met Ben of S33 Home Team. He's the social coordinator for Scott's group. We suggested our home teams meet for dinner.

Satan is attacking my mind. He has me feeling insecure about things I said to James and Ben.

James responded to my email two days later. Do I sit and wait, Lord? Do I encourage him, since he hasn't dated in a long time?

November 3, 2007

James was in Houston and Chicago the past 7 days and broke a finger (flag-football). He admitted that, due to his divorce, he is gun-shy. I think he needs time to heal, so I suggested we remain friends. **In my heart, I know he's not going to date me now, if ever.**

It's Saturday morning, and no word from James. His kids are number one and his job is number two. I would be number 3 or less; I'm not sure that I can handle that.

Help me, Lord, release any frustration or disappointment. Two activities in two months and no phone calls—he's not interested. I pray for my Christian husband.

November 10, 2007 [Touch Down]

I finally did it! God gave me a chance to talk to Scott and I took it! He was on his motorcycle about to leave. I walked up and said, "Is your name Scott?" He looked over, removed his sunglasses, and said yes. "Hi, I'm Charlotte. I believe our home teams are having dinner together next Saturday." We proceeded to chat for a few minutes. Turns out he lives a few streets away from me!

January 3, 2008

Thank you for my evening with Ben last night. I appreciate his friendship. He made me laugh out loud several times.

Dear Lord, I pray for Ben's future wife; may she have the noble character of a true woman of God. I don't know if that woman is me or not. I also pray for my Christian husband; may he cultivate the qualities of Christ in his life. Amen.

January 4, 2008 [Answered Prayer]

[A high school student had keyed the hood of my Maxima while I was parked at school.] I prayed God would perform a miracle regarding my car repair. After pleading with Service King and my insurance company [to cover the full cost of repainting the hood], Service King agreed to remove the additional $125 fee for repairing the preexisting rock chips!

January 13, 2008 [Promise from God]

I'm still struggling *in my mind* with the slow pace of Ben's friendship. I need to be content with what we have and not yearn for more. It's not Ben that my flesh craves; it's a relationship—the romance, attention, and thrill of falling for someone.

I'm still holding on to your promise, Lord, that I don't have "much longer to wait for marriage." I know your definition of "long" and mine are not the same. It will be one year in May since you spoke that to me. [*] I trust you! Help me be loyal to you and let me die to my selfish desires.

[*One night in May 2007 I was watching TV at home. I leaned forward to adjust a pillow and suddenly heard, "You don't have much longer to wait." I froze while the spirit within me said, "For what?" The voice replied, "Marriage." This was the first time *God* had spoken to me, apart from Holy Spirit promptings, *and* He confirmed I would marry!

An exciting part of this miracle that I failed to record was what happened a few days later. I received a mail-order *wedding* catalogue from a company I've never bought anything from! It was the *only* mailing I've ever received from them, and yet my full name and address were printed on the mailing label. This was not a chance coincidence; it was God revealing Himself to me in a personal and intimate way. Oh, how He loves to surprise us!]

January 18, 2008

I dedicate this day to: **Loving myself and God, who made me.**

No more pity party—Satan, you are going down!

Twenty-five things that are great about me (in random order):

1. chemical engineer
2. salesperson
3. teacher
4. dancer
5. sense of humor (funny)
6. tenderhearted (empathetic)
7. hardworking
8. loyal
9. dependable
10. beautiful
11. great figure (ooh-la-la)
12. pretty smile
13. silly
14. love to travel
15. speak German
16. welder (how many blondes can say that?)
17. love to write
18. good housekeeper
19. gracious hostess
20. kind neighbor
21. sense of style
22. generous
23. thoughtful
24. classy
25. woman of God!

January 22, 2008

I must make space between Ben and me—mentally and via email. **Unmet expectations and faulty thinking are to blame.** The Holy Spirit instructed me to back off and see if he pursues. I cannot force anyone to love me. I will wait and pray for strength.

Thank you, Jesus, for your peace that fills my heart! You shaped me this weekend by breaking me down and putting me back together. New and improved Charlotte!

January 26, 2008 [Dating Wisdom]

I dedicate this day to: Lessons learned the hard way.

I want to remember: When God says "no," we need to let go. (Trying to understand *why* will cause confusion and frustration.)

This is the last time I'll reflect on my brief friendship with Ben. He's never contacted me, so here are my lessons learned:

1. Allow the man to initiate contact. Do not shorten the chase.

2. Allow the man to plan an activity and extend the invite.

3. Allow the man to email first, even after a date.

February 2, 2008

February 14 is around the corner and I think I'll invite some girls over.

Heather, Vanessa, and Emily are engaged and Tamar is pregnant. **Some days I struggle with the feeling that everyone else is moving ahead with their lives and I'm stuck in "Single Land."** I know the Lord is developing my character in this time of waiting and trusting.

Help me, Lord; guard my heart. I don't want to ride the "Excitement and then Disappointment Express" each time I meet a new guy. I must protect my heart and mind to stay grounded in future relationships.

February 24, 2008 [Evidence of Healing]

I dedicate this day to: God's Holy Spirit working in me.

Someone who inspired me: T.D. Jakes, "God's got you covered!"

I want to remember: God's faith and love growing inside of me.

I can be a stronger person tomorrow: Continue mediating on Scripture and Joyce Meyer teachings.

God, you are amazing! How you have healed me (and continue to move in me)! I ran into Ben leaving the worship center on Friday after T.D. Jakes spoke. I was alone and he looked straight at me and smiled. I smiled back with a peace that I didn't have the last time I saw him. The Holy Spirit prompted me to hug him so I did. I'm thankful the Lord restored my confidence, which allowed me to show sisterly love to someone who hurt me. Please continue to work in me supernaturally!

Then on Saturday night at church, I ran into James. We've been out of touch since December and we chatted a few minutes. He asked if I would be interested in playing tennis again and I said yes.

It was incredible to see two guys that I once felt rejected by being so welcoming, *and* I was at peace during our encounter. I will view them as casual friends. I appreciate the shift in my thinking and pray to maintain this healthy view.

March 23, 2008 [Struggle Resumes]

Oh, Lord, my heart is heavy and my slumber light! I passed Ben at church with a female and my heart tightened. I smiled and said hello as he hugged her. Ben never sat with me at church. I thought my insecurity was gone—dead and buried. What changed?

Oh, heal me, Lord. Let me cooperate to receive your love, mercy, and forgiveness. Let me lay my burdens at the cross. Help me to empty my head. Why can't you take him away?

Move him to a different church or city? Somewhere where
I won't see him again? **Probably because you want me to
grow—to forgive and forget.**

Right now, I feel so mixed up inside. I'm unsure where to
volunteer and whether to continue hosting home team. I can't
distinguish my fleshly desires from spiritual promptings. I
continue struggling with my selfishness and confidence.

March 30, 2008 [Growing Pains]

Why do I feel anxious at church? Why is it hard for me to
smile and be joyful when I'm with my home team? I cannot
explain what I'm feeling, but something's going on. I've
noticed a lack of words—it's happened at church, at school,
and with friends. It's like the joy from my heart has been
removed and there's an empty vacuum.

I'm playing tennis with James at 10:00 a.m., home team is
at 3:00 p.m., and my parents arrive at 6:00 p.m.

I've been struggling for 3 months with the changes at
Fellowship and our home team. I don't know if I want to
host anymore. I'm confused, Lord! Help me, because I don't
understand my emotions. **I assume I am growing and it feels
awkward.** Change → conflict → growth.

April 15, 2008

I want to remember: Freedom comes from trusting God for all
my needs and concerns (church, school, and dating).

As I press on, positive changes are taking place. I've
committed to playing tennis this year, and God continues
sending me people who play.

Summer is 7 weeks away.

It's awkward being in the transitional phase. Some of the
"deadness" or lack of joy has departed for the moment. If I
can stop thinking about me and focus on others, then things
will settle into place. **Having peace is being calm and
confident (in God) in the midst of turmoil.**

April 19, 2008 [Anger and Resentment]

I dedicate this day to: Living in victory.

Prayer: Cast off every hindrance so you may run the race that God has set before you. Run to win the prize! (1 Corinthians 9:24).

I'm tired of struggling, disappointment, and lack of control over my thoughts. I want to walk in victory every day, and yet yesterday I crumbled. I broke down after first period because I had become angry at a student and then frustrated with the class. I had prayed for God to calm me and control the words from my mouth. I pour so much time and effort into explaining the science concepts well, and yet I couldn't get my words out.

I need your help, Lord! I want favor with my students, coworkers, and administrators. I want to be full of joy, peace, and confidence. I don't want to beat myself down.

I realized that I have hardness in my heart. I resent Fellowship's decision to discontinue our singles class and create a service for "thirty and younger." What about thirty-plus singles? Then Ed did a series, "Just Get Married," stating men should marry in their twenties, and there's no such thing as a soulmate—there's more than one person. But isn't there only *one* whom God has chosen as "His best?" I want to be on fire for my church. I don't want to be bitter, but I feel abandoned. All I can do is pray for my attitude to change. Sometimes I wonder if I should visit other churches.

April 26, 2008

I'm excited and full of joy! This week, God has renewed my spirit and grown my faith. The pressure has lifted as I released my fears and worries to Him. I want to feel like this forever! **To be anxious about nothing starts in the mind.** Joyce Meyer's *Power of Thoughts and Words* has really helped me.

I'm at peace with home team since confessing my concerns to the leaders. A healing occurred, and I think I'll stay with them.

May 8, 2008

Something that brightened my day: A student commented that when I stand in front of the projector, my earrings sparkle and give off rainbows. [*] The kids in 7th period thought it was cool.

[*Rainbows are a symbol of God's promise to never flood the whole earth again (see Genesis 9:12-16).]

I went to the class "God's Will" in a great mood, ready to meet new people. As I came up the stairs, Scott walked by. He sat 3 tables away; and as the night progressed, I grew restless. My thoughts were bouncing between Scott and the lady next to me, who was annoyingly happy and peppy. By the end of class, I was struggling with contentment.

May 26, 2008

I dedicate this day to: "It's raining men! Hallelujah it's raining men!"

I want to remember: Arriving by myself to an event and expecting to be alone.

What a neat day! First, the drive-in movie yesterday was a blast! We parked next to Scott and his home team friends. I met Henry, who is type "A," like me!

I volunteered today at the volleyball tournament. James arrived at lunchtime with his boys. Earlier I chatted with Jason, Vince from Zurich, Will, Tom, Greg, Henry, and Nate. It was raining men!

June 1, 2008 [Wrong Thinking]

I dedicate this day to: Being still and spending time in prayer.

I had fun with James and his boys at the pool. It's hard to keep my feet on the ground and head out of the clouds. Feelings can be deceptive, but I'm falling for James.

Lord, keep my focus on you! Keep my thoughts and motives pure. My feelings seem to be lust driven. **I repent of these selfish daydreams.** He is my brother in Christ until further notice. Redirect my thoughts and guide my steps.

June 9, 2008 [First Spiritual Fast]

I dedicate this day to: Fasting for those who are lost, the impact of Fellowship Church in the world, and a renewing of my mind and body as I focus on Christ.

Day One of Fast—I'm tired and hungry; today is liquids only. I bought ninety-two dollars' worth of organic groceries.

James picked me up to play nine holes, best ball. After church, a group went to see *Kung Fu Panda* and I sat next to James. He helped me with a flat tire in the parking lot and followed me to a gas station. I hugged him to say thank you, and it was there at the Shell station that he kissed me for the first time!

June 10, 2008

I dedicate this day to: Fasting and salsa dancing!

Blessings I'm grateful for: Food—mainly carbs.

Day Two of Fast—It's past midnight, and I have energy! I volunteered for four hours at Fellowship in the Pre-K building, and then James picked me up for salsa lessons. I had a blast. He kept me laughing half the night!

June 12, 2008

Day Four of Fast—I met Warren [welding friend] for lunch. I ate black beans, salsa, and guacamole, which are all "okay." I only ate 3 chips, 3 strips of chicken, and 3 flour tortillas that are "bad." We talked for 3 hours at Uncle Julio's. He said it's a good sign that James and I are spending every other evening together and that he calls when he says he will.

June 15, 2008

Today is Father's Day. I'm framing a photograph for Dad. I'll take it on the plane along with Mom's teapot.

The food fast is over, but now we're fasting from media to spend more time with the Lord. I may fast from TV, although I don't watch much.

June 16, 2008

I dedicate this day to: Leadership!

Prayer: "Go and make disciples."

Tomorrow is the last day of the Plano Leadership Team Leader Academy. I'm learning a lot. I feel out of place with all the "super teachers" and their years of experience or natural ability. Teaching is unnatural for me. I force myself to learn new skills, and I want to be relaxed and confident with classroom management. I want to be a strong team leader for IPC [Integrated Physics and Chemistry], and pray to handle the increased responsibility well.

July 6, 2008

Prayer: When I'm weak, God is strong. Help me be strong when I need to be!

I want to remember: **Lust is powerful. It's like a drug that messes with your mind.** All logical reasoning is out the window, during and after the encounter.

I can be a stronger person tomorrow: By setting boundaries and enforcing them.

July 12, 2008

I dedicate this day to: Living by the power of the Holy Spirit.

Prayer: Sin is no longer my master! I'm free, by the blood of Jesus!

Something that brightened my day: Quiet time with the Lord.

I want to remember: **My flesh may be ruling my life more than the Spirit.**

James and I chatted on the phone several times. He returns Friday. His boys may do Adventure Weekend, which means I get James to myself. Is that selfish? I've only seen him two hours the entire month of July.

July 20, 2008

Something that inspired me: The movie *Radio*. It was part of the church message on compassion.

James picked me up Friday for pizza and a beer. We drove to Grapevine for the Summer Nights concert and sat in lawn chairs, ate watermelon, and listened to country music. Saturday, James and I played tennis and went swimming. We reunited at church and sat together for the first time.

July 23, 2008 [Dating for Marriage?]

I want to remember: Do not listen to voices that create doubt, fear, and worry. **Be aware of truth versus a story I tell myself to explain someone's actions.**

After realizing James and I haven't had any serious discussions other than "no sex before marriage," I woke up worried. I emailed my concerns, including 3 personal traits about me. [Upon receiving his response, I realized that] I had falsely believed he wanted a wife, someone to care for him and his boys. My heart aches at this realization.

Dear God, quiet my heart and fill me with peace. My mind's racing. Why is this complicated?

July 27, 2008

Something that inspired me: *Les Misérables*—Jean Valjean was shown grace by a priest and later extended grace to his enemy.

I want to remember: **Whether a relationship starts or ends, God never changes.**

James called after his boys went to sleep. He's not ruling out the possibility of remarrying, but he's doubtful he'll be able to trust again.

I care deeply for him and know he doesn't love me at this point. I must protect my heart from jumping to conclusions. Even if James and I date for a year, it won't mean he's ready to marry. I may be taking a risk of continuing, knowing there's a chance he won't be able to love me.

August 17, 2008 [Holy Spirit Warns]

As I dressed for church, I had a sense that something was wrong. **It was the Holy Spirit preparing me for what may lie ahead.** James said he'd call but didn't—not Friday or Saturday. It was odd and the first time that he didn't follow through. I went to church and sat with my home team while he served communion. After the service, James turned toward me with empty eyes. He was robotic and distant. I asked if he felt all right and he said yes. I told him he's not acting his normal self and inquired about his blood sugar several times, thinking that may be the reason.

August 20, 2008

Today is the 3rd day of teacher in-service. James and I spoke on the phone 3 nights ago. I brought up last Saturday— something was off, and it really bothered me. He didn't realize that he acted differently.

He's supposed to call this week [and today is Wednesday].

August 21, 2008

I dedicate this day to: Waiting for James to call, Part II (this happened last week?!?).

Prayer: All things work for the good of those who know and love our Heavenly Father.

My mood has changed on this second day of my period. All week I was happy and peaceful. Today, I'm selfish and worried about James. He said he'd call but hasn't. I don't want to be frustrated that he's not keeping his word. This makes two weeks in a row.

(Over one hour and twenty minutes later . . .)

James called!

August 25, 2008

I had fun with James and his boys yesterday.

Today was the first day of school. I felt peace all weekend and throughout the day. I pray for strength and confidence as I continue setting the tone this first week.

Thank you, Lord, for all your help and guidance today! ☺

September 14, 2008 [Family Fun]

Last night after church, James and the boys and I went to Steak 'n Shake. It was my first time and I had so much fun! We played games on the kids' placemats. I wore a paper hat and ate my first steak burger. It was memorable—the four of us laughing and being silly!

September 22, 2008 [Lost is Found]

Something that brightened my day: Watching a dollar-theater movie with James while eating gummy bears, holding hands, and laughing!

I left my wallet at the Kroger checkout—a lady ran after me in the parking lot! Thank you, Lord, for returning it to me! Cash, credit cards, I.D. all there!

October 7, 2008

I dedicate this day to: Being sick (again).

Prayer: If God brings me to it, He will bring me through it!

Something that brightened my day: Getting a "☺" on my teaching evaluation.

October 10, 2008

> I dedicate this day to: Healing from strep *and* a bad reaction to antibiotics.
>
> Prayer: This too shall pass.
>
> Blessings I'm grateful for: Walking, sitting, and showering after 3 days.
>
> Something that brightened my day: Flowers from James on my birthday!
>
> I want to remember: My neighbors went to CVS for me. I was too sick to sit up, let alone drive!

October 14, 2008

> Today was a struggle. Two IPC tests are missing—did I grade them? I have too much on my mind with behavior issues, CoGAT testing, a new chemistry unit, and papers to grade.
>
> I'm cranky about James not calling. He rang Saturday, chatted ten minutes, and said he'd call later; I expected Sunday night. Monday and Tuesday came without an email or phone call. We haven't set my birthday dinner yet.

October 26, 2008

> I dedicate this day to: Letting go and letting God take over! I will do what God asks me to do; I will give God what I cannot do. No matter what, I will trust God.
>
> **I cried at church, on and off the entire service.** I'm sick again after being healthy for two weeks. I'm frustrated. This is the 3rd time since September! Am I overtired and stressed from the demands of teaching?
>
> Lord, please make me well! I have too much to do to be sick *again*!

December 11, 2008

> Something that brightened my day: James brought me chicken soup and Tylenol.
>
> I have strep throat again!

Please, Lord, don't let me get it in the spring! I've missed five days for sickness and one day for car trouble. Maybe I need gloves when I touch student papers?

December 23, 2008

I sent James an email last night with a series of questions: Am I your girlfriend? If so, then why do I want to see more of you than you want to see of me? He called a few minutes later from Target and we talked for over two hours. I was really hurt [by a number of his past actions]. He apologized, but I'm still disappointed at how little I will see him before his kids arrive. Oh well, it's not up to me as to how he spends his time.

January 2, 2009 [Medical Emergency]

I called 9-1-1 for the first time. Last night, I arrived at James's just before 7:00 p.m. I noticed the porch light was off, which was odd. The boys were playing Wii, and James was in the shower. I played two games, and by 7:30 p.m., the shower was still running. Jokingly, I asked his oldest son to check on him "in case he passed out."

James didn't respond to, "Dad? Dad? Dad!!!" So I went in and saw him lying at the bottom of the shower, passed out for real! He was up to his neck in cold water with shampoo bottles floating around! I shut the water off and opened the drain. James was shivering and unconscious. I dialed 9-1-1 on the house phone, but it was dead. I took out my cell, and his oldest son told the operator the address while I covered James in two large towels. Four paramedics showed up in 3 minutes. The men administered glucose, and he came to fifteen minutes later.

When the men shouted James's name repeatedly to bring him back, the boys left the room. Concerned, I went after them. The oldest son was on his knees and looked as if he was about to pray. I asked if I could pray with them and gave them a chance to add their own prayers at the end. I was a bit shaken too.

Everything turned out all right. James was back walking around, yet very cold to the touch. He was mad at himself that he [allowed his blood sugar to dip too low].

February 7, 2009

Back aches, chills, headache, and exhaustion—I can barely stand on day 3 of my viral infection.

February 12, 2009

Lord, please help me right now! I'm so mad at James. . . .

February 14, 2009

Today is Valentine's Day. I have a boyfriend, but the problem is, I don't have any plans. James never mentioned getting together. He called around noon, but I didn't answer; instead I started crying. I was at Walmart seeing V-Day stuff everywhere—roses, candies, balloons, chocolates, etc. I feel worse than a single person on Valentine's Day. At least I have no expectations when I'm single.

James emailed me yesterday to apologize for not calling about the singles class. I replied, "Thanks for the email. I forgive you." Less than twenty-four hours later, I'm mad again. **What's the real issue here?** I think it's that I don't feel special or important to him.

February 19, 2009

I dedicate this day to: Waiting on the Lord.

I bought myself flowers for $3.99 at Kroger—red-and-white mix of mums, daisies, and carnations. I just really wanted flowers.

Mom asked about Valentine's Day and I told her what happened; she found it odd. Four friends saw more than one red flag, but Nisa and Renee (who know me best) told me to keep watching and pray. They were more forgiving.

God allowed us to start dating. When I prayed "The Dating Prayer," James was still there. [The prayer from 2002: "Lord,

show me the truth about ____. Bring us closer together or
farther apart." Whenever I've prayed it in the past, the guy has
faded away rather quickly].

March 3, 2009 [Seeking Discernment]

I still have my eyes and ears wide open. I'm praying for God
to reveal the truth about James. Is he capable of loving me like
Christ loved the church? Is God his priority?

March 6, 2009 [Truth Revealed]

Lord, please give me a calm mind and heart! James and I spoke
for an hour after singles class. I feel we are unequally yoked.
That was the topic tonight. **Dating a Christ follower is not
enough; we must be seeking God with the same *intensity*.**
The advice was to break up if the intensity is unequal.

I told James [of my concerns]. The "grand finale" was
spring break—a red flag went up when he planned a ski
vacation without inviting his girlfriend of eight months. He
pointed out how cold I get and how the twenty-degree temps
would make me miserable. It was a load of crap. I gathered
my stuff slowly and opened the car door. I stepped out, and
said, "I can't believe that you wouldn't want me to be there." I
closed the door and walked to my car. James didn't come after
me. No apologies. No phone calls. I didn't sleep well for half
the night.

Today I emailed Renee to pray for me, and she left a sweet
message. I pray for my Christian husband!

March 28, 2009 [First Spin Class]

The week after spring break went well; I gave new seating
charts. There are two weeks until report cards, and over ten
students are failing; I need to finish calling parents.

I took a spin class this morning. The instructor Laurie had a
gel seat that I borrowed, and a guy named Dong helped me set
up my bike. I survived the class, but my legs are like Jell-O.

March 29, 2009 [Reconciled]

I never mentioned what happened with James. I called him on the 21st and left a voice mail. He called back and apologized for not inviting me on his trip and to his boys' sports games. It hurts to feel like an outsider to his daily life. James wanted to continue the relationship, but I had doubts. I keep praying for direction.

April 1, 2009 [Unsettled]

I dedicate this day to: A twelve-hour migraine!

I want to remember: Raising your voice and talking louder are two different things.

Dear Lord, my migraine has gotten worse as the day has progressed. I pray to lay down *all* of my burdens and worries.

Today is Wednesday. Since seeing James on Saturday, he finally emailed to ask if we can meet for dinner tomorrow. If I go, will I break up with him? Or will I give him one more chance?

April 9, 2009

James came over, and I spilled it all—I'm an outsider in his life, he's too busy, he's not crazy about me, the Valentine's Day disappointment. I told him that I don't want to force him to move in a direction that he's not ready for, but I cannot be his part-time girlfriend. I was prepared to end it but didn't. **Whether it was the Holy Spirit or a moment of weakness, I gave him one last chance.**

April 12, 2009

I dedicate this day to: Easter—Christ's death, burial, and resurrection.

James invited me to over for Easter dinner. I brought cheesecake and strawberries for the boys and turtle fudge brownies. After dessert, we did an egg hunt in the backyard, and the boys presented me with Easter lilies and a basket of chocolate bunnies!

May 5, 2009 [Pattern Repeats]

Well, James did it again! I'm very upset. . . . I sent another email today. He replied 3 hours later with no remorse, just "blah, blah, blah." I left him a voice mail asking for an apology.

I'm praying for discernment. Should we take a break to hear from God more clearly?

May 7, 2009

2:28 a.m.

I listed James's priorities in order: family, work, Charlotte.

The ones I'm looking for in a man: God, me (as future spouse), family, work.

We met for dinner last night to talk. I said that he's married to his job and his work is more important than me. He explained things are busier and he'll have less free time this summer. I told him again, "Your job is more important to you than I am." Again, he said nothing. Believe me, I paused long enough.

I think it's over this time. I should've stepped away on Valentine's Day, but I forgave him, as Christians are supposed to. The past four months we've had four discussions about his priorities and my needs. The same issues repeat over and over. I prayed for God to take James away if he's not The One. He hasn't.

Lord, help me let go and transition back into singleness.

9:36 p.m.

Praise God for His strength and confidence to face a new direction. I haven't told James it's over, but I will pray about how and when. Renee has been supportive, calling me several times. **I feel her prayers, and God has given me grace to be at peace.** It will be difficult integrating back into a home team that barely exists. I haven't seen them in 3 weeks.

Maybe I'll join eHarmony when school's out. I want to be with someone who thinks the world of me. I know he's out there! Bring him my way, Lord!

May 9, 2009

3:15 a.m. [Interference]

I can't sleep. My emotions and thoughts are all over the place. On the drive to school, I was deciding what day to break up with James, and then a wave of emotions came over me, and I started having second thoughts. **I can't tell truth from lies right now. My judgment is cloudy.**

Why do I keep a record of all the times James has let me down? The Bible says that love keeps no record of wrongs and it doesn't force its way. Is the problem with me? James *has* made improvements, and there is evidence that he's making an effort to give me what I want. But the issue of work and communication remain. I want more of his time on the weekends, but he's been working. Should I be more understanding?

3:47 p.m. [Interception]

I talked to my brother for over an hour. When we hung up, I felt better. I felt I could give it another chance, so I called James to ask if he wanted to meet after his game tonight. He said sure and asked where. For some reason, I tensed up and felt uncomfortable. I asked if I could ask him a question, then I choked up. **Nothing came out of my mouth, but tears streamed down my face.** [The Holy Spirit was interceding to redirect me.]

There I was, planning to move forward with James, but something was obviously bothering me. Maybe it's the fact he was willing to watch me walk away. He's not that crazy about me. *That's* the real issue, not his work schedule.

May 12, 2009

I booked my flight to Michigan for Nisa's wedding. I have over 170,000 airline miles, enough for two first-class tickets to Europe for a honeymoon. Not knowing when that will be (marriage), I should start using my miles now.

9:35 p.m.
Lord, I hate to confess it again, but I'm upset. Is this the voice I should listen to regarding James? Or is this the selfish, whining voice? Maybe the lesson is to not use email to discuss anything important (feelings).

May 23, 2009

James and I reconciled the day after my last entry. He apologized for not responding sooner. I realized that I had a choice—be angry that James didn't respond the way I wanted, or be forgiving and full of love. In the future, I should *not* discuss delicate matters over email. It's too agonizing.

6:50 p.m.
Am I going insane? Well, I can't bear to give all the details. James has hurt me again. Am I the problem? Whenever I forgive him and let the wounds heal, he tears them open.

May 24, 2009 [Finally Finished]

It's finally over. As of 3:00 p.m. today, James and I spent two hours on the phone having the same conversation, and he apologized as he has done so many times before. We agreed that he can't give me what I want. What I've always known has proven true: he's not crazy about me.

I feel like a fool for dating a man who doesn't love me. What lies am I listening to, hoping that one day he's going to wake up and realize that I'm wonderful? What's wrong with me?

God, help me release *all* of my memories and forgive James. He did not intend to hurt me. I am an awesome woman of God who deserves to be loved by a true man of God. The best is yet to come!

I've lived my life the past few years in a way that honors God. **I stumble here and there, but the Lord knows my heart.** I want to follow God's will for my life, and that means letting go of James.

I pray for peace and confidence as I live my life as a single woman of thirty-two. Make me content with my circumstances, not bitter or resentful of those who are married, engaged, or having children. My time has not come.

May 27, 2009 [Adjusting to the Loss]

Day 3 after the breakup—deleting pictures and emails. I pray that I won't see him for a while; I need time for the emotions to settle. Maybe I'll attend the Sunday service where I won't know anyone. No pressure of being asked, "Where's James?"

Overall, I am coping well. Sometimes I wonder if Clay [from Lincoln training] will turn out to be God's best for me. We're good friends, but I haven't felt the spark.

May 28, 2009 [Learning from the Loss]

This morning was tough, but the day got better. I erased more emails and reread some saved ones. One talked about finding a biblical mate, another was Cheri's perspective on my relationship with James. She had strong convictions that his behavior was unacceptable, and her husband agreed. I'm mad at myself for not ending the relationship sooner.

May 31, 2009 [Grieving the Loss]

I went to the 10:00 a.m. service with a tender heart. The music stirred up emotions, bringing tears to my eyes. I don't know if I'm grieving the loss of James or the loss of friendships. **I know many people at church, but I don't know who my friends are.**

Lord, help me heal and move forward with joy. I pray for godly friendships that will minister to me and keep me heading in the right direction.

June 8, 2009 [Hugs from God]

It's wild how 3 guys asked for my number within a twenty-four-hour window!

June 14, 2009 [Mental Attacks]

Satan has been after me in the past twenty-four hours. I had bad dreams and negative thoughts about several people from church, including James.

June 16, 2009 [Another Hug]

I'm at DFW waiting for my flight to Michigan.

Super Shuttle picked me up in a silver Lincoln Town Car with tinted windows and leather seats! I sat in the back like it was my own personal limo! I had expected the big blue van.

My back's been bothering me. This may be the year I see a chiropractor.

June 17, 2009

We leave for Mackinac Island tomorrow. Dad's driving, and we'll stop for a picnic on the way.

I hoped leaving Texas would leave behind memories of James and his boys. I guess not. It's hard to keep the faith and keep my spirits positive. Everything will work out in the end, but I still feel discouraged. All of my high school and college friends are married and Nisa's engaged. Amy's sister (3 years younger) had a baby boy. It's hard to not feel like I've been left behind. What is God waiting for?

Lord, help me to be content with my singleness. Help me make new friends and get plugged in to a home team. Let this time in Michigan be a time of rebuilding.

July 2, 2009

I had a nice flight back to Dallas. I sat next to a Canadian named Aaron who was on his way to visit his girlfriend in Fort Worth. We chatted as we walked to baggage claim. It was nice to meet someone new, if only for a moment.

July 8, 2009 [Ceramics Bust]

> 5:28 a.m.
> Too much on my mind! I signed up for ceramics at a local community college. I feel apprehension at the duration of each class, four hours and twenty minutes, but I guess starting anything new is a bit scary.
>
> I hope to finish my eHarmony profile this afternoon. They matched me with 7 guys in my area. I think I'll join for 3 months. There are *few* prospects at church right now, although I've stopped looking. They need to find me!
>
> 6:47 p.m.
> Ceramics didn't go well. **Everyone else loved it, but I struggled.** I could barely hear or see the instructor and fell behind shaping ten balls of clay. Everyone finished except me, and we moved on to make ten pinch pots from the clay balls. She gave us ninety minutes to do it, and walked away! I only made 7. Then the instructor picked one piece that she liked from everyone's collection—everyone's *but* mine! She must not have liked any of mine. That's when I realized I may not come back.
>
> When I got home, I dropped the class. Last night, I had a feeling that something wasn't right and I asked the Lord, "Was I not supposed to sign up?" I think I got my answer.

July 13, 2009 [Memories]
> I've thought about James for the past few days and added him and his boys to my prayer list. Not sure why he's on my mind. I'm struggling with a strong desire to communicate with him. It makes no sense.

July 16, 2009 [Moving Forward]
> I'm meeting Alex from eHarmony for shaved ice tonight.

Last night was dinner with a home team friend. She's doing well, but her job is moving to Wisconsin. She doesn't want to move but is scared to find a new career. I can relate, recalling my transition from sales to graduate school to teaching. Along the way I struggled and worried that I had made a mistake. Now my [3rd year] of teaching is behind me.

At Dallas Life Foundation, I fed the homeless with S25 Home Team. It was a positive experience; I handed out Diet Cokes.

July 26, 2009 [Dating Epiphany]

I realized something through eHarmony: **I need to be spiritually, intellectually, physically, and emotionally attracted to a man in order to date him.** It's not easy to find a man who fits those criteria. That's why I don't date much.

August 4, 2009

Alex invited me to dinner on Saturday. I was reading my Bible and talking to God about contentment. I prayed for my Christian husband and my cell phone rang—it was Alex!

August 9, 2009

4:12 a.m.

I can't stay asleep—my mind is swirling from my date with Alex. He was seated at a table at P.F. Chang's and stood up when he saw me enter. He didn't sit down until I was seated. I was impressed.

August 20, 2009

Today is the fourth day of teacher in-service. The building construction is far from done, but the hallways, bathrooms, and classrooms should be ready. Praise God, my classroom wasn't a disaster!

Alex met me for dinner and we talked for 3 hours!

August 23, 2009

Last night, I saw James at church. I waved and gave him a one-arm hug. After the service, Wendy and I went outside to Family Fun Fest, where we ran into James and his boys. I stopped to chat but sensed the boys were uncomfortable seeing me again. It hurts to think they were hurt by my disappearance; they are too young to understand dating.

August 31, 2009 [Mental Attacks]

First week of school is history! The Lord took my fears and gave me peace. I slept well the night before—a new record!

Now that the easy week is over, I'm stressing. My shoulders are tight and I wake up around 3:00 a.m. and can't fall back asleep. **Satan's messing with my mind. The battle has begun!**

September 5, 2009

Alex picked up tickets for Sunday's "Picnic in the Park." The Dallas Wind Symphony will perform, followed by the movie *E.T.* I'm excited!

Second week at school went great! The stress lifted and classes are balanced.

Apparently, eHarmony is running out of matches for me. I knew it had to happen! I have one more month prepaid, through October 7.

I turn 33 this October! That's the age Jesus [was when he died on the cross]. I still long to be a wife and mother; but now that school's in session, I have little time to think about that, except when I have a tough day. All in God's timing.

September 12, 2009

I'm feeling better from my cold, but Alex didn't call. I thought we were having dinner tonight. I remember him saying, "We can plan on it." Did I misunderstand? Did he forget??? I went to church with a heavy heart, after having a tough Friday at school.

I'm drinking a Jack and Coke now. I'm very disappointed, since he knows that I'm leaving town next weekend. I guess he doesn't want to see me. I want to know what happened. **I prayed the Holy Spirit would remind him of our dinner plans.** Although tentative, he should've called!

September 15, 2009

I was right—Alex is not interested in dating me. I got a confirmation via email. He still wants to be friends, but I don't see that happening. It's over.

I'm in contact with 3 other guys on eHarmony. Not much else to say. Two days of school, and then I get on a plane for Michigan.

September 20, 2009

Yesterday was Nisa's wedding in Bay Harbor. Several high school friends were there, and 3 of them joined me at my table. I cried tears of joy, imagining how awesome Nisa must feel to have Jeff to spend her life with. My turn will come. I pray that I cooperate with God, as to not prolong the process!

A friend's mom and new husband were there. They met on Match.com several years ago. It can happen that way, but I'm doubtful that's what God has for me. I don't want to renew my eHarmony membership. **I want to invest time in the Lord and restore my passion that was so strong when I first believed.**

September 27, 2009 [Brother Attends Church]

[My brother and nieces came up for the weekend.] We watched a DVD last night and went to the 10:00 a.m. service at Fellowship Church.

October 10, 2009

Tonight Wendy and I are meeting for dinner and a live performance of *Mary Poppins* at Fair Park Music Hall.

I closed my eHarmony account. Two guys are emailing me at my Yahoo address.

Henry [from church] and I decided to dress as "Tony and Jessica" for the costume party. I got the blonde wig, pink jersey, and large sunglasses for my head (as a famous picture of her shows).

October 15, 2009 [Post-Birthday Blues]

One guy from eHarmony decided not to pursue because he doesn't like my church. The other guy hasn't responded. It's God's way of stripping my life and dating options to nothing. That's how I feel—like nothing. I don't know why my heart is heavy. Most of my adult life I've lived without dating. Why does it feel so lonely and disappointing every time a guy lets me go?

Steff and Nisa both forgot my birthday. The science department didn't give cards this year. Oh well, life goes on. **People will always let you down. That's why our faith is in the Lord.**

October 18, 2009

I skipped home team and spent an hour reading and praying. I feel more fulfilled, and I know that God's working in me during this time of rebuilding.

October 24, 2009

The "Jessica and Tony" costume was a hit! I only talked with Henry during check-in and near the end of the night. He's social and flirty; I don't know what I think about him. He likes being the center of attention.

October 25, 2009

Well, I missed my 9:00 a.m. meeting because my digital alarm clock thought it was Day Light Savings. It jumped back one hour, and I rushed to the 10:00 a.m. service. Then I volunteered at singles class selling tickets for the picnic.

Henry waited for me to finish so we could eat together. Afterwards, he invited me out for ice cream.

October 31, 2009

Tonight was the Halloween party. Henry greeted me, gave me a hug, and disappeared. The next time I saw him was an hour later, talking to a group of women about a haunted house. I caught the end of his story, and then he left to check on the pizza. Eventually, Henry sat down and we started talking.

After two minutes, a guy walked in with a tall blonde. Henry turned and with great excitement said, "Michelle! You came!" The two of them began talking and walked off without a glance or a word to me. I felt somewhat neglected. After a few minutes, I walked into the kitchen. A moment later, he walked in with her and I didn't look up—I took more pudding and fled the room. I inhaled the pudding, all the while hearing a voice in my head telling me to "Get out of there, fast!"

As I started to leave the party, Henry said, "Leaving already?! You just got here!" I turned and flashed a fake smile, waved goodbye, and kept walking. I didn't pause to say anything or to let him finish—was he finished? All I know is that I felt hurt and unimportant. I was there two *hours* and got two *minutes* of his time.

November 1, 2009

Day Light Savings gave us one more hour today. I slept all right but woke up frequently. I still had some hurt and anger toward Henry.

I saw him after the singles class today. **With the Lord's guiding, I decided to talk with him in person before leaving.** We walked outside and I told him, "I'm sorry for getting mad." He apologized for not spending more time with me. I thanked him for calling last night and for his voice mail. Our conversation was balanced, both of us taking turns talking and listening.

Lord, take captive my thoughts and make them obedient to you. Fill me with your peace, joy, and love for others.

November 3, 2009

Part of me wants Henry to pursue, and the other part hesitates. I really don't have much in common with his friends. That may be a red flag. If I don't have much in common with his friends, do I have much in common with him? I know the Lord will reveal His will and whether we should date. No emails or phone calls since seeing him Sunday. Today is Tuesday.

Protect my heart, Lord. "Do not arouse or awaken love until it so desires" (Song of Solomon 3:5 and 8:4 NIV).

Henry just called. We're on for dinner Saturday.

November 6, 2009

My period starts soon, and my emotions are more dramatic: fatigue, frustration, and feeling overwhelmed. Some days teaching is such a struggle. I wish I were married. Sometimes I feel like I'm being punished because God won't give me what my heart desires. **I know that's my flesh talking. It always wants the easy way out.**

November 15, 2009

Last Sunday was a dark day. Something snuck in and stole my joy and peace after singles class. It was a type of restlessness, a fear of something. Henry's group went for burgers and I didn't have peace about it, so Wendy and I met up for lunch. I still didn't feel right. My guess is that I experienced spiritual warfare or hormone levels off the chart.

December 3, 2009

Henry's mom passed away and the funeral was today. I'm praying for his family. I cannot fathom what it feels like to lose a parent and realize you won't talk to them again, or hug them. **Thankfully, she was a Christian and is in heaven with Jesus.** There must be comfort in knowing that, considering the alternative of hell.

December 6, 2009

Here it is again—the gray funk that returns before my period every 30 days. One month ago, I had the worst meltdown ever on the phone with my mom. It must be hormone related, more than spiritual warfare.

I told Henry that I don't have much in common with his female friends. I'm confused how they can love the Lord and yet go out drinking at a club on a regular or semiregular basis. What's weighing on my heart now is how Henry doesn't seem to hear me. When I speak, I don't feel validated or understood. I pray that God will make it clear to both of us if we should continue dating.

Lord, I need guidance. Are you telling my spirit that something's off, or am I overthinking and listening to my feelings, which are often deceptive?

December 31, 2009 [3rd Christian Boyfriend Breakup]

New Year's Eve—who really cares? Henry and I ended our courtship on the way home from Austin. It was a 3-hour drive back to Dallas. I slept the first hour, and then slowly, we revisited our [unresolved disagreement from the previous night]. Too much was said and my feelings were hurt when he went into "lecture mode," telling me how rigid I am and how I need to be more flexible, etc. I warned that he needs to be more tactful when pointing out other people's weaknesses or faults. He seems to lack sensitivity in that area.

I am worn out—emotionally and physically from lack of sleep! I realized [through the Holy Spirit] that Henry was unaware of his words and how they were being received. I forgive him because he "knows not what he is doing."

January 2, 2010

I spoke with my brother for two hours today about dating and Henry. In the end, whoever was at fault for "this or that" doesn't change the end result—we are not a good match, and that is okay. I forgive him for his rampage of verbal accusations and want to stop replaying the scenes in my mind. **I realize that to move on and refocus, I must stop talking about it.**

Did I tell you that I got a Christmas card from James? He wished me a Merry Christmas and a good school year. "The boys say, 'Hi, Miss Charlotte!'"

This is a New Year—may it be focused on God and others. I don't want to be selfish or inflexible.

Lord, *please* change me unless you want me to stay as I am! Only you can change me, and I believe that you will. It may take longer than I'd like, but you will do it!

January 3, 2010 [Reflecting]

Mom and I are reading *The Purpose Driven Life* together. We will email or talk through the discussion questions. It's a forty-day commitment.

Looking back on 2009, I see much personal heartache. The first four months were peppered with struggles with James and the dying relationship. I finally ended it in May, and I was heartbroken, mad, and confused. In July, I joined eHarmony and dated Alex for a month before he ended things. Next was Henry, who didn't seem to know if he wanted to date me. There were 3 breakups in the last six months, and I have learned a lot.

January 11, 2010 [Mental Attacks]

It's 1:30 a.m. I had a great week living with my purpose in mind, but now I'm dealing with spiritual warfare. It started during the singles class when I sat alone in the back after volunteering. Henry was there and I felt uneasy. I was at peace with him in my mind; but when I saw him, I tensed up. He said hello as he walked by. I smiled back but wanted to flee. I hate feeling insecure! Did I believe Satan's lies again?

Today was an off day. I continued struggling at Dallas Life Foundation, while serving the homeless. I cried on the drive home. Why? Even now, I can't sleep; my mind is not at rest. Lord, help me!

January 16, 2010 [Ask and Receive]

I booked my Rick Steve's Tour of Italy. God led me through it! My first flight option was 132,500 miles [airline points]. Returning through Detroit was 152,000 miles, which was more than I had, but I could pay $300 to buy extra miles. A few days later, I called back. **Before I dialed, I prayed that God would pair me with the right agent to assist me with the right flight.** He connected me with a girl who previously lived in Lewisville, Texas! [That's where I live.] She located a return flight from Rome to Dallas with a 7-day stayover in Detroit for *less* than my original itinerary! It was 115,000 miles, *plus* I'll stay in Detroit to see family and friends! A double blessing! And there are 27,000 miles remaining, enough for another flight! I'm excited! Thank you, Jesus!

Wendy and I will celebrate her birthday, and then we'll stop by a fundraising party. James and Henry are supposed to be there—my two exes! Thank goodness, I'm at ease with James after seeing him at church and receiving his Christmas card. Soon Henry will have harmless passage in my mind.

January 17, 2010 [Feeling Faint]

I feel so mixed up and restless on another Sunday. I went to church and singles class alone. I don't know why I find it so discouraging.

As soon as we arrived at the party last night, James was to my left and a female friend to my right. I froze, not knowing who to talk to first. I chatted with Henry in the kitchen and suddenly needed some water. Ten minutes later, I felt faint and nauseous! I sat on the balcony for fresh air, thinking I may

pass out or throw up. Was it from anxiety, having James and
Henry in the same room? Maybe God (or Satan) wanted to get
me out of there. Once we left, I started feeling better.
**God, help me stay sane during this time of upheaval
and rebuilding.** I feel like a renovated house—my insides
are gutted and will be replaced. I don't know how long this
will continue. Give me what I need to make it through with as
much joy and peace as possible!

January 24, 2010

Today is the first Sunday in weeks (or longer) that I wasn't
depressed leaving church. I emailed a prayer request to several
friends. **I'm praying for a committed group of friends to
share life with, whether at Fellowship Church or another
church.**

My massage therapist invited me to join her at The Village
Church.

I will keep praying about whether I should restart my
commitment to home team.

February 6, 2010

Last Sunday, two home team friends were supposed to meet
me for service but didn't show up. Nor did either one call or
text or email. I was disappointed but chose to not be offended.

I emailed my massage therapist several days ago about
attending her church but haven't heard back. I don't know if I
should go to Fellowship or to The Village in the morning. I'm
seeking God's direction, but He may not have a preference.

I've been disappointed in the attendance of the thirty-five-
plus singles class. It's a revolving door of different faces each
week.

February 12, 2010 [Seeking Change]

Snow day! Dallas got over 7 inches of snow. We haven't had
this much snow in thirty years!

Wendy and I went to a Super Bowl party and left after half-time. I decided that I do not want to attend any more parties where Henry will be. I can't seem to relax and enjoy myself.

Mom and I finished our forty-day journey through *The Purpose Driven Life*. Yesterday was the last chapter! **There's so much about me that needs to change. I want to be more like Jesus.** I want to be content and joyous in all circumstances—every day at school or home or wherever! I want peace and love for others, and I want to be a good representative for God. I find myself battling feelings of rejection, selfishness, and disappointment with people. My mind needs to be renewed, and I need God's help to change!

I need direction if I should stay at Fellowship. I missed church and singles because I joined my massage therapist at The Village. I've also thought about visiting Irving Bible Church.

I wish change happened overnight so I could have all the fruit of the Spirit when I wake up tomorrow and be an entirely new being on the inside! **But I've learned that God uses people and events to test us, grow us, and change us little by little as we obey Him.**

Joyce Meyer has been teaching about being relentless and determined. If you're willing to hurt and be patient, and hurt and be patient, you will eventually press through to victory! That's where I am now—hurting and trying to be patient.

February 20, 2010 [God Speaks!]

I watched *Fireproof* last night. My massage therapist wasn't there, but I recognized two of the ladies [from The Village Church]. I met Erica, a twenty-four-year-old who's going to Czechoslovakia to teach English. She likes ballroom dancing and needs single friends too.

Since the ladies did not directly invite me to church this weekend, I will visit Irving Bible Church. I need to decide whether to go to their main service, the singles class, or both. I want to start slow and keep expectations low. Disappointment occurs when there's a large gap between our expectations and reality.

On Monday and Wednesday nights I felt God leading me to let go of Fellowship. Brian Houston is the Pastor of Hillsong Church in Australia. His Monday broadcast was about letting go of dead works. **Something God has blessed for years can change; God moves from it, and we tend to stick with it, not realizing we need to let go.** God used that message to confirm that He wants me to find a new church home *and* He wants me to lay down Fellowship completely. I asked God, "Do I continue serving at singles every other weekend [while visiting other churches]?" His immediate reply was, "When something's dead, do you let go completely or partially?" As Joyce Meyer would say, "Revelation!"

Two days later I watched Joyce [on the same channel]. She confirmed that obeying God usually means giving up something, and that it will be difficult in the beginning. She addressed our fear of what people may think when stepping out in a new direction. That was another revelation—my fear of disapproval from the church staff. Joyce warned that there will be opposition and we will have some lonely nights ahead; but if we spend time with God each day and obey Him, we will make it through to victory. **Along the way, we must ignore our emotions and listen to the truth of the Word.**

I'm so grateful for Joyce Meyer! God bless her, and bless me on my new journey! Give me strength to not be afraid! Amen.

CHAPTER 9

INCREASING ALTITUDE AT IRVING BIBLE CHURCH

MY SPIRITUAL JOURNEY BEGAN at Fellowship Church when I was a young adult searching for peace and purpose. After receiving Jesus Christ as my Lord and Savior at twenty-five, my life changed forever. I received my first Bible, joined my first Bible study, and made new Christian friends. I began serving and tithing at church, and I even changed careers from technical sales to teaching high school. As I paused to pray and seek God's will for my daily life, the Holy Spirit began prompting, counseling, convicting, and guiding me.

As I matured as a Christian, I encountered spiritual warfare—resistance from the enemy—mainly in my mind. The enemy also stirred up trouble during important life events. I received my first Bible, and a few days later my car window was smashed and my workbag was stolen. My company's demo van was broken into and two welding machines were stolen during the *same* weekend of my baptism. These are not random coincidences, but rather evidence of the unseen spiritual battle that takes place around us.

In addition to spiritual warfare, I also experienced answered prayers and miracles. My first miracle happened at the Raleigh-Durham airport. It was also the first time I remember praying instead of immediately panicking in a stressful situation. God responded by sending an airline employee *directly* to me, despite the long line of people. Not only did I make my flight, but I was upgraded to the bulkhead row! When I landed, the second miracle happened at the Dallas–Fort Worth airport. I needed change for a ten-dollar bill, so I asked God to send me someone. Seconds later, my prayer was answered! I was so excited! My faith grew leaps and bounds that day.

One of the greatest miracles, I believe, is when God Almighty speaks directly to us. He often communicates through the Bible, His Holy Spirit within us, and through people in our daily lives. As you read in the previous chapter, God had spoken to me twice up to this point in my life. In both instances, I heard a voice inside of my mind, clearly not my own, and every cell in my body froze. These divine encounters encouraged me greatly and increased my confidence to trust God and follow after Him.

During my eight years at Fellowship Church, I evolved from a nonbeliever to a church attender, to a new believer, to a follower of Jesus. I experienced significant spiritual growth, and yet I still had a lot of sin in my heart and mind. By the end of 2009, I encountered a spiritual dryness that caused me to draw closer to God. After several months of praying, waiting, and struggling, He led me to a new church home to continue my journey.

My next spiritual chapter begins at Irving Bible Church.

March 1, 2010 [A New Beginning]

>A new month, and spring is on its way to Texas.

>The last two Sundays, I attended Irving Bible Church. There was prayer time while the 7 Deadly Sins were displayed one at a time. The first sin was anger—I cried. Recently I realized that I have anger issues, not just my dad. **But with the pain of realization comes the promise of forgiveness and the healing of the Spirit.**

>God has blessed me with peace and joy since I obeyed Him by leaving Fellowship. A weight lifted. A chapter closed.

>Yesterday my neighbor Dana joined me for service. The topic was fasting, one of the spiritual disciplines. I was moved by the message and music. After the message, we spotted our neighbor Michelle, and Dong from spin class! I was very encouraged.

>Last night, I met Erica for dinner and we spent two hours talking and sharing. I'm thankful for our new friendship.

March 7, 2010

>Thursday was open house at school; I was so tired Friday that I thought I may fall over! We had standardized testing on Wednesday, and a cheating circle was revealed after a chemistry test. Twenty students were identified, and two were in my class. It's been a lot of drama and stress.

>I went to IBC [Irving Bible Church] alone today. Dana wants to come again and bring her daughter. I'm excited that she's excited about church.

April 2, 2010

>Today is Good Friday. I'm at the Nissan dealership getting my rotors cut. My car is now ten years old. With the new fence and Italy trip this summer, I'm hoping for my car to hold on another few years.

>Mom and I are talking about attending the Joyce Meyer Women's Conference in St. Louis this September. It would be our first mother-daughter getaway. I pray it works out.

I signed up for two classes at IBC. One is "Bible Reading and Reflection." The other is a four-week class called "Propel" for newcomers.

April 8, 2010 [Mental Attacks]

I feel Satan battling the Spirit in my mind. Yesterday I felt run-down and weary. Whether it's hormones or spiritual warfare, I'm in unrest, discontent, and discouragement.

The two IBC classes start this weekend. I desire true fellowship with other believers. I want to marry and have a family, but I'm learning to be content.

Help, Father, my soul is burdened. Lift me up and restore my peace, joy, and confidence in Christ!

April 13, 2010 [Big Blessing]

I went to Joyce Meyer's book signing! Erica and I took the day off and drove to Legacy Books. Joyce signed while her husband Dave sat next to her. I shook their hands, introduced myself, and her assistant took our picture. I purchased 3 books—one for Wendy, Mom, and myself.

The grading period ends Thursday, and many students are close to failing. I'm thankful the end of school is approaching.

My table leaders at Propel were former singles from Fellowship Church! We will meet 3 more times, and then I'll visit Thrive for singles in their thirties and forties. Dong will join me.

I'm enjoying my life right now, even the quiet Friday and Saturday nights. God is doing a work in me, and I see some progress. **I have a greater awareness of my sin and when I say or do something wrong.** The devil is quick to condemn, but I repent and ask for forgiveness.

April 27, 2010

Mom arrived Friday night. On Sunday, we went to IBC for the service; Mom loved it! She liked the songs, the message, the

Chatter magazine, and the café. Dong joined us for service and bought us a coffee afterwards.

After church, Mom and I had lunch and then stopped at Borders bookstore. She bought a Parallel Bible with the King James Version (KJV) and the New International Version (NIV) both on the same page. Later we watched Dr. Charles Stanley's program on TV.

May 14, 2010 [Challenges]

Many things are weighing on me, and I need to cast them all on God:

1. Interwrite pen intentionally broken by 3 students
2. Worsening student behavior in all classes
3. End-of-course field testing that I did *not* volunteer for!
4. Teaching 3 weeks without Interwrite [electronic tablet]
5. Students failing
6. New fence construction delayed
7. Busted water pipe at my faucet (can't run soaker hose for foundation)
8. Volunteering for the first time at IBC

May 21, 2010

A long week at school has ended.

My Italy trip is approaching! I don't think I'll have time to learn Italian.

I volunteered at IBC's Single Parent Carnival and visited Thrive the next day. **I was really under attack at Thrive and wanted to be alone.** I wasn't in the mood to mingle and did not join them for lunch. I hope this Sunday goes better.

I started *Battlefield of the Mind* last night, a gift from Erica.

May 22, 2010 [Unplanned Surprises]

Pentecost Sunday! Today is the anniversary of the church, as recorded in Acts. The Holy Spirit came upon the people, and many spoke new languages! I didn't know about Pentecost.

I joined Thrive for lunch. Barry sat across from me; he plays tennis. A few others do too.

Renee's going sailing this summer. She called to say that we'll be in Rome at the *same time*! We will also be at the Rome airport at the *same time*, but on different flights! God will determine our steps. Craziness! ☺

June 6, 2010

Friday was the last day of school. I had 3 IPC and 3 chemistry failures. I stayed late to paint over the vandalism on the lab tables.

I went to Thrive's missions dinner last night. Part of me is interested in [a guy from Thrive], but he said that he doesn't get much out of the worship at church. It makes me question if he's close to God. I find the music very moving and penetrating. It gets my heart and mind ready for the message. It gives us time to redirect our thoughts from our schedules to the Creator of the universe.

June 10, 2010

I leave in 3 weeks for Florence, Italy! I'm excited but also nervous.

I met Bruce from Thrive to help with his job search. We drove to 3 learning centers. Next week, we'll visit schools to drop off his resume. His car doesn't have AC, so I offered to drive.

Erica's fundraising sale is June 19. I offered to donate items and work the sale.

Rick Steve's tour group mailed a list of participants. Everyone in our group is a family, a couple, or sisters, except for two guys who are traveling solo and me. I pray these guys become my "tour buddies" during our free time! If not, I pray for a family or couple to adopt me into their group!

June 14, 2010 [My Yoke to Bear]

Church was powerful—"God is a God of Plan B." We make plans and live our lives as if they were our own. Often we are disappointed with challenges, setbacks, illnesses, etc., that come our way. Once again, I realized that my life is so blessed. I have struggles against Satan, his lies, and disappointment about being single in my thirties, but my life seems easy compared to those who suffer real losses. Thank you, Jesus! **If waiting to be married is my yoke to bear, that's not that bad.**

Saturday is Erica's garage sale. I emailed and passed out flyers at church. I'm praying that God will provide people to *work* and people to *buy* so she can raise her final amount.

June 20, 2010 [Mental Attacks]

Today is Father's Day. I wept in singles class during prayer requests. Mine was regarding my dad and brother, who don't know the Lord. That's all I wanted to say, but the table leader probed further. If he had sensed my discomfort and moved on, I may have suppressed the flood of tears that engulfed me! I was mortified, unaware these emotions were buried. The group was supportive, though I feared their judgment. **Satan was all over me, filling my thoughts with fear of rejection and inadequacy.** Strangely our class message today was on fear. I learned at Fellowship Church that many of my issues are a result of fear. I had no idea!

Lord, show me what to do, in addition to prayer, for my father and brother. I'm not the light I once was to my family. I'm more mature but less passionate. Some of "old Charlotte" has returned. As I read in *Battlefield of the Mind*, I pray for release of strongholds and exposure of false beliefs. My thoughts aren't always true, and I must fill my mind with the Word.

June 26, 2010 [Answered Prayer/Obedience]
Erica raised $1,083 at her sale! That was my desire, but I didn't know if it was possible. **God provided all the people—a steady stream for four hours!**

God placed it in my heart to buy Rosetta Stone language software for Bruce. He plans to teach Spanish and get certified. The desire came Tuesday after driving him to local schools. I got excited about blessing him with something he couldn't afford. When I realized Levels 1-3 cost $539 and Levels 1-5 cost $699, I was stunned. I prayed but did not act.

The next day, my internet service was repaired and I checked email. One of the *first* messages was from Borders containing a coupon for Rosetta Stone—saving $125 on Levels 1-5! I felt the Holy Spirit nudge, "Do this." Thirty minutes later, I turned on Joyce Meyer. **The topic was obedience—obeying God, no matter what!** That was it—I drove to Borders immediately and bought the last one.

The following day I met Bruce to give him the gift. I didn't hear from him until later, because he was struggling to accept it. I pray God has revealed what he should do—I assume open it and get started.

July 30, 2010 [New Addiction]
A month has passed since my last entry. Bruce kept the software and is on Level 3.

I was in Italy for eleven days and met Renee in Rome. I got asked out by 3 Italian men: a twenty-year-old, a thirty-year-old, and a forty-year-old! ☺ I wrote about my trip in a separate journal.

Since being back, I started a scrapbook, met Clay for church, volunteered at IBC, and met David [who was also volunteering].

I joined Facebook and am now addicted. As a new member, I have a lot of friend requests. Jake found me! I accepted his request, and we've been in contact for 7 days. He's unmarried, no kids, and living in a different state. I'm praying for his salvation again.

I've been watching Joyce Meyer in the mornings and then spending quiet time with the Lord. I'm working on listening more [and waiting for Him to speak].

August 11, 2010

It's 2:00 a.m. and I can't sleep. I talked to David for forty-five minutes. I finally found the words to describe him—it's like *I already know him*! We've been out twice, but I feel closer to him. He left a message about going to the World Aquarium and I was so excited, I couldn't sleep. So, date number 3 is Saturday.

Gosh, I'd hate to be wrong, but I think he may be The One! Too soon to know, but I'm praying God will guard my heart and direct our conversation.

August 26, 2010

I had a great day with David.

This was the best start of the school year! I slept well and was more relaxed. I interacted with students more intentionally and felt more confident in my ability to teach (with God's help, of course!). Many friends are praying for me.

Nisa was baptized Sunday at her church in Michigan!

David invited me to join him and friends on a road trip. They will float on the river and dine at the Gristmill. The plan is to leave Saturday at 6:00 a.m. and return around midnight. Even though it's a crazy thing to do after the first week of school, I'm pretty sure I'll do it!

September 6, 2010

I went with David and his friends—a four-hour drive plus four hours on the river. We ate breakfast in Waco, and our next meal was at 9:00 p.m. Instead of driving back, we crashed at Nigel's apartment. I slept on an air mattress, but not well. No ear plugs, no change of clothes, and one guy snored! The trip was fun but exhausting.

I'm hosting a Labor Day cookout today. David and Wendy are coming, plus twenty-five from Thrive.

Yesterday was a great message on becoming a disciple of Christ, Luke 14:25-35. **I must love Jesus more than my family, friends, and myself. He must come first.**

(Ten hours later . . .)
The caffeine in my Jack and Coke is keeping me up. I'm disappointed how today turned out! The cookout was 1:00 to 6:00 p.m., but the bags of ice didn't arrive until 2:30! By then, someone had bought some at CVS. The cooler arrived after the ice; buns and ketchup didn't make it until 3:30; and David showed up after 3:00 p.m.

The whole day was stressful. I had fun for a while outside in the quiet. Someone counted over forty people. Drinks, desserts, an unsliced watermelon, and more were left behind. Why does it bother me when people leave their stuff? If I won't eat it, I feel pressure to give it away. I was nearly in tears when the last person left.

September 9, 2010 [Feeling Blue]
It rained all day Tuesday and Wednesday. Both days were a challenge—I felt depressed. David has not called since seeing him on Tuesday. Tomorrow is Friday and we have no plans to do anything, just like last weekend. Maybe he observed flaws in my personality during the road trip and while I was hosting my (stressful) party.

Lord, this doesn't look promising. The frequency of his calls and our dates is decreasing. I guess I have to wait it out and pray. If he's not The One, then "he" is out there somewhere.

September 14, 2010
To my surprise, David called last night. I didn't pick up because I was eating dinner and watching Joyce Meyer. If he can take a full week to call and not see me all weekend, then I

should have a week to call him back. If he shows persistence, then he's seriously interested.

October 2, 2010 [Hug from God]
This journal is from the Joyce Meyer Women's Conference. Mom and I attended five conference sessions, and near the end, an usher asked if we wanted to move to the front. We were rewarded *front and center* second-row seats for the final session, when Dr. Caroline Leaf and Joyce spoke! It was great!

I enjoyed Dr. Leaf's discussion on the human brain. We build "green, healthy trees" or "ugly, black trees," based on how we think. Our mind controls our body, and toxic thoughts cause physical and mental illness over time.

I'm really struggling with student behavior this year. So are other teachers in my department.

October 9, 2010 [Turning Point]
I've learned so much about myself in 2010. **The Holy Spirit continues to reveal sin in many areas—my mind, mouth, and mood.** As Joyce says, I'm grateful when the Spirit convicts because it allows me to go to God in prayer, ask for forgiveness, and be changed by His love. The process is slow, but I believe He's doing many great works in me. I am aware of my selfish and critical spirit.

An incident occurred in fifth period. I called the school office to have a defiant student removed—no one came. I sent an email fifteen minutes later—no one responded. When class ended, I called our secretary. No one responded to my urgent email, not even by the end of the day *or* the next day! The dean of students eventually came by to apologize. This is the second time I've been in a critical situation and she didn't show up.

I don't know what to do, but my eyes are on God! I'm fighting to keep a positive attitude, while feeling mistreated by students and staff. Humility is perfect quietness of heart. It is to be at rest when you are blamed or despised. It is to take no offense about how you are treated (paraphrased, Andrew Murray). Maybe this is the lesson?

October 31, 2010

Last night was the Thrive Halloween party. I was Athena the Greek Goddess, but I was in a funk earlier and almost stayed home. **Each weekend, I feel more worn and less desire to be around people.** After two Jack and Cokes [*] and some Metallica, I got in the party mood and put on my costume. I'm glad I went.

[*This was one of only a *few* instances where I was so low that I turned to alcohol to elevate my spirits since becoming a follower of Christ. Christians are to seek the Lord for all things and turn away from worldly idols to ease our pain.]

November 1, 2010 [Mental Wellness Day]

I'm taking the day off to check Christmas airfares, read, clean, and have quiet time with God. I also have papers to grade and notes to prepare. I want to enjoy this day of rest without feeling guilty. I pray for peace and quietness of spirit. I pray for a good sub report. I pray for strength to take one day at a time and to enjoy the journey.

Father, my heart is heavy. The burden I carry is too heavy; I give it to you. Help me to seek your approval more than the approval of coworkers and administrators. Lord, I need you to fill me with your mercy, grace, love, joy, peace, and righteousness! I receive these gifts from you now.

November 13, 2010 [Shut Down]

Right now I hate teaching. I can no longer do labs with fifth period. I shut down the lab, and two boys rolled on the floor laughing. Literally! The class couldn't behave in their seats for long. A female student with anger issues warned the boy who sabotaged the lab experiment to stop taunting her, then she stood up and punched him in the stomach. It was awful!

I give up, Lord! I'm at the end of my rope. Things are worse now that [two boys] are back from in-school suspension. My fifth period is wild. I cannot force them to do anything, and neither can the dean. I'm quitting before Christmas. I may write my letter this weekend and take off Monday. I hate fourth period now as well. I put a kid in the hall for twenty minutes. It's been intolerable this week; I didn't know it could get any worse.

Lord, help me out of this pit of moral destruction! Give me grace to finish the last 30 days with a right attitude.

November 24, 2010

Today is Thanksgiving. I'm thankful for warm clothes, family, friends, and God working in my life.

I went to Thrive's Thanksgiving dinner. There were about twenty of us singles.

I'm not sure if I wrote about this, but Derek from church asked if I'd like to take dance lessons. We have been learning the Argentine Tango over the past four weeks. It's such a blessing—a stress reliever and joy booster. He invited me to join him at Boston Market after class. I guess it was a minidate.

December 5, 2010 [My Second Resignation]

No emails or texts from Derek. I must release it into God's hands. It's not about what I want (selfish Charlotte!); it's about what God has planned for my life.

Friday, I placed my resignation letter in the principal's mailbox during 7th period. I expect to be called into her office. I pray for strength to stand strong—no tears, please!

Lord, slow down my mind and mouth so I can walk in your Spirit regarding school and my personal life. Help me be content where I am in my career and singleness. This teaching job does *not* define who I am, and neither does any guy's rejection. I am a child of Christ, designed to be someone great. *God loves me no matter what!*

December 8, 2010 [Supernatural Miracle!]

Last Thursday, I had decided to turn in my resignation because I was becoming a monster and cried twice at school. **I prayed at my bed that night, on my knees, for God to confirm that I'm doing the right thing by leaving now.** I went to bed and awoke to the sound of music in my room at 4:00 a.m.!!! It wasn't the clock radio (set for 5:30), but my nativity scene snow globe with music box that Mom gave me years ago! I had not wound it in over a year, but it played the last verse of "Silent Night": "Sleep in heavenly peace, sleep in heavenly peace." I took that as God's confirmation that I was doing the right thing.

I didn't fall back asleep, and part of me was scared by the music playing in the dark, on its own; but then I sensed it was God. *On December 3, 2010, God answered my prayer in the most creative way!* I'm so thankful for that! Not sure where I am to go, but I will walk and pray for God to direct my steps.

I have 7 teaching days left. I don't want the students to know until after I'm gone.

December 12, 2010

Dr. Leaf's office responded to my October email! There is a position in their new Dallas office opening January 15! I revised my resume and Renee is reviewing it.

The situation with Derek is a mess in my mind. Tuesday he's hot and Sunday he's cold. Last week, we talked at Boston Market for the second time. We laughed and hugged goodbye. I could have sworn he said he'd be in touch this week— nothing!

I pray for God's protection over my heart and strength to perform well at school. I pray for the manifestation of the dreams God placed in my heart (Dr. Leaf job, tall women's clothing line, **write autobiography**, travel). Good things are headed my way! Thank you, Jesus!

December 17, 2010 [Another Transition]

Today marks the end of a four-and-a-half-year chapter in my life; "Ms. Benke," the high school science teacher, is no more. My last day was marked by excitement, anxiety, awkwardness, silence, and sadness. I am sad to leave the few students who really like me. I am sad that I couldn't become what I wanted to be. I am sad other teachers are impacted by my decision.

An unusual thing happened today—five students stopped by to show their appreciation. One gave me a Starbucks gift card, two former students wished me a Merry Christmas, and two others gave me a big hug, one on each side. They said I am "the best chemistry teacher ever" and "We love you." I couldn't tell them I was leaving. They'll find out when they pick up their schedules in January.

I had emailed the principal about working January 3, the teacher workday, because we still had not met in person. In fact, she was gone when I went down to turn in grades, and so were the other two administrators. None of them wished me well or spoke about my leaving.

I got emotional turning in my keys and badge. Olivia the janitor helped me load my belongings into my car. I cried on the drive home as the realization "I'm done" became real. I don't doubt the good things God has ahead. I'm mourning the loss of a four-and-a-half-year career plus one and a half years of school, which is six years toward a dream that didn't turn out.

God has a plan; it may be my "Plan C," but it's always been His "Plan A." I'm grateful for my time at Smith High School and the lessons learned. I'm not a natural teacher and do not enjoy working with rude and disrespectful teenagers.

Over the past five days, I have doubted that I did the right thing. When I read Scripture or watch Joyce Meyer, I wonder if God intended me to stay and suffer. But then I remember my prayer for confirmation and my music box playing. **I will cling to the truth of that moment when my mind is confronted with doubts.**

Tuesday was our final tango class. Derek walked me to my car and asked if I'd like to have dinner on Friday. He called to reschedule for Monday; I was disappointed but assumed it was best. Being alone tonight and journaling is really good for me now.

December 28, 2010

My time in Michigan went well. On the 24th, we had our big dinner at 3:30 p.m., and then opened presents. On the 25th, it was just my parents and I, so I stayed in my pajamas the whole day! Mom and I watched *Oprah's Favorite Things* and Joyce Meyer's interview with John Maxwell. He spoke on being thankful and expressing gratitude to others.

January 1, 2011

Happy New Year! A group of us went to the Dallas Symphony for a NYE performance, *From Paris to Vienna*. The music was incredible!

I met Derek for lunch to clear the air on several issues. Despite our date, he's not ready to date me. I also apologized for something I said on Facebook that was directed at him.

January 4, 2011 [Answered Prayers]

Today is my first day of unemployment. Yesterday I helped my replacement teacher prepare for IPC. I prayed the night before to not be emotional and for students to not be in the building with their schedules. Both prayers were answered! Thank you, Jesus!

Last night, I skipped dinner and prayed for the Dr. Leaf job opportunity.

I'm reflecting on 2010 and the New Year with many ideas: **write an autobiography**, take a cooking class, take tennis lessons, read a book on Martin Luther.

January 11, 2011

I'm enjoying my time off.

My LDL cholesterol is too high. The doctor said to exercise more, and no diet change was necessary. I have been exercising 3 times a week.

Last week, my neighbor Dana was outside wearing a cast on her arm. I pulled over to talk. Her girls came over to play, and then I went to her house for four hours! Her husband worked late, so I stayed to open jars for her and assist with dinner. We sipped wine and hung out. It was *so nice*! **Unplanned fellowship like that rarely happens.** I am a planner, and my job takes the life out of me so that I don't want to be around people when I get home. Dana was grateful to have me over, and I was grateful to be there. What a blessing!

January 20, 2011 [First Commitment to Pray]

Who would have known that I would stay so busy during my 3 weeks of unemployment? I'm not having time to write in my journal.

Dr. Leaf's office was collecting resumes and will review them this week. Friends at Thrive are praying for me.

I got my car's state inspection done. While waiting, I met the finance director of a medical staffing company in Irving. They are hiring six people to start in February.

I watched Joyce Meyer, went to the gym, and spent time praying and waiting for God to speak. My roommate from my 1997 summer internship called to share about her mission and calling to reach Muslims in India. I committed to pray every Wednesday.

It's Friday night, and I'm spending time with the Lord. **I want to read more, study more, learn more, and live it out.** I want to finish *Battlefield of the Mind* so I can read more books!

January 26, 2011

Week four of unemployment isn't as fun as previous weeks. God has been pruning things out of my life, starting with dating. I followed up with Dr. Leaf's office, and I don't have the experience they are looking for.

Let's recap: Derek was pruned off Monday and Dr. Leaf was pruned off Tuesday. I'm staying positive and allowing my faith to remain stable. **Pruning precedes growth!** I'm in a time of waiting on God. I'm thankful for this time of reflection and study in His Word.

My final paycheck at school was almost $2,000 more than I hoped! Praise God!

February 1, 2011 [Godly Approach]

Mike from Thrive called on Sunday. I barely know him, but he called to say that he appreciated my help. He went on to say that he has noticed how I interact with others and finds me to be kind, sincere, generous, humble, and empathetic. Not only was I surprised that he liked me, but I was also *blown out of the water* by his approach. Mike believes dating is a precursor to marriage and would like to get to know me through dating. **He recognized qualities in me and valued them enough to want to date me.** I've never had a man tell me those things! I have long desired to be seen as a "pearl of great price."

February 10, 2011

I made minipizzas for the Super Bowl party. Of course (ha ha) Derek was there, which surprised me. No one knew Mike and I came together until we left after halftime.

Today Mike and I went to Starbucks to work on his Bible study. When we got to the temptation verse, it led to my issue with lust. We talked about it and prayed together.

February 16, 2011

UPS delivered a box of chocolates from Mike!

I had some ladies over for Valentine's Day. By 10:00 p.m., I was so ready for bed! Mike called and said to look out front—

he was getting out of his car with a red rose! He stayed for two hours.

I'm thinking about enforcing a curfew because I haven't slept well the past five days. **We talked about setting boundaries, and I should follow up to make sure we're on the same page.**

February 21, 2011

I applied for 3 jobs online and I emailed my resume to Rosie [church friend] regarding a contractor position at her workplace. I had bumped into her Thursday night at Fellowship Church when Wendy and I went to hear Joyce Meyer! [I met Rosie through the women's summer Bible study at my house in 2007.] **It was my first time back to Fellowship Church, almost one year from when God told me to let go.**

March 4, 2011

Monday, Mike and I watched a funny movie at his apartment. He hardly laughed, and I realized that we don't share the same sense of humor.

Wednesday, I had a phone interview. The manager had twenty-three candidates and wanted to invite 3 people for a formal interview. If chosen, I would receive a call. Guess what? I got called! I can't believe *I made the cut*!

I'll continue praying that God closes doors that I shouldn't walk through and opens right ones. He is in control of my job search.

March 9, 2011

My Keirsey personality type is "INTJ"—Introvert, Intuitive, Thinking, Judging. I am 67 percent introverted and 89 percent judging. People with my personality are best suited for careers as a design engineer, research scientist, computer programmer, environmental planner, law, and librarian. Notice how it doesn't say sales or teaching! This confirms what I already sensed; certain careers are not good for me! And that's okay! We are all made differently! **INTJs want people to make** *sense*, **which often causes frustrations or social setbacks because we are so rational.**

March 13, 2011 [Lights Out]

It's 9:20 p.m. I went to bed early after calling Mike twice and leaving two messages. I needed time alone and wanted to forego our movie plans. We had spent all weekend together, and I had been out of the house eleven hours today. I was overtired and emotionally unavailable.

To my dismay, Mike didn't listen to my messages and drove to my house. He rang the doorbell after I had turned out all of the lights and gone to bed with my ear plugs. Since I didn't come to the door, he knocked on my bedroom window, which freaked me out and made me very angry! I let him know it when I opened the front door.

March 16, 2011

We kept our plans to visit the Arboretum [but things were strained]. Once the tears started, I told Mike that I've wanted dating boundaries since the start. I had asked him earlier if we needed a curfew and if we're spending too much time together. He didn't think so, but I did.

I felt better after our talk but woke up at 3:00 a.m., aware of new wounds. **I don't know if it's spiritual warfare or the Holy Spirit warning me.**

April 1, 2011 [Answered Prayer]

Mike met me for church on Sunday and things were strained [because of our conversation the previous night]. He prayed at the altar in place of communion, and I knew he was struggling with us.

I visited a family friend and his parents in Frisco this afternoon. I had a nice time and told them about my new job. I had received a call on Tuesday of last week to schedule an interview the next day at 3:30 with CGC, a financial services contractor. [When I had bumped into Rosie at Fellowship Church when I went to hear Joyce Meyer, she had told me about an opening at CGC. Rosie passed my resume on to a recruiter, who happened to call on Tuesday while I was watching Joyce Meyer!] The CGC interview was in the *same* building as another company that I interviewed with! God must want me there! I interviewed with 3 managers, and at the end, they made me an offer to join their team! The paperwork was emailed before I left the building. I start on April 11 with 3 weeks of [case advocate] training.

The following day I was prepared to break up with Mike— but his conviction was so strong that I doubted if it was right to end it. Maybe I'm focusing on his flaws (or differences) instead of his strengths (godly man, loving, great with kids, hard worker, servant, expressive, thoughtful).

I pray that God will reveal the truth to both of us. Are we right for each other?

April 10, 2011

I met Clay for dinner and we talked until midnight! The last time I saw him was in October. When I think of Clay, I think of a friend with whom I share much in common. We've been friends for 13 years! If it is your will for us to be a couple, change our hearts, Lord, so we will feel that way about each other.

The next day, Mike and I broke up after volunteering at IBC. [Our personality differences and boundary issues repeatedly clashed, causing friction and continuous misunderstandings.]

April 13, 2011 [My 3rd Career Begins]

Monday was my first day at CGC. I joined the group of trainees waiting in the lobby. Minutes later, the finance director of a medical staffing company entered the building. He remembered me from the car inspection station in February! I told him that I hired on with CGC on the sixth floor! He's on the 7th.

There are twenty of us in the training class. I ate lunch with
Rosie and chatted with Stuart from the interview. Glen from
the interview came over and shook my hand. It felt good to be
recognized by four people on my first day! Thank you, Lord!

April 23, 2011 [Mental Attacks]

Training is going well, although last week I was under spiritual
attack regarding my ability to perform to their expectations
(i.e., few mistakes, quick turnover). I also had some anxiety
about Mike. Thankfully, I feel stronger in both areas. **God has
me at CGC for a reason, and maybe for a season.** I won't
know what His plan is; all I can do is *trust* and *obey*!

The Good Friday service at IBC was profound and
emotional, as we relived the arrest, trial, beating, and
crucifixion of Jesus. He died so we may live with Him for
eternity in heaven. **Jesus took *my* place on the cross and was
bruised for *my* iniquities and took all of *my* sins upon him.**
I'm forever grateful for what He has done, and my soul weeps
for the awful suffering He endured.

Thank you, Jesus, for going to the cross. Thank you for
loving us enough to give up your life. Thank you for your
mercy, grace, and love. Fill me with your Spirit and your love
so that I may share it with the world around me. Give me
wisdom and discernment. Let me see people the way you see
them. Fill my mind with understanding and my heart with joy.
Allow me to walk in confidence based on who I am in Christ!
I will make mistakes and people will misunderstand me. I'm
not a pleaser of men but only want to please you, Jesus! Help
me renew my mind so I can carry out your plan. Amen.

April 30, 2011 [More Attacks]

Week 3 of training is over, and I don't have my assignment
yet. It's tempting to feel like the "bottom of the barrel" when
other trainees were placed immediately.

Thursday was a rough day. My coworkers were loud and inconsiderate of others trying to get work done. Nearly half of my class was chosen for Craig's new team—receiving the *big* work areas on the *quiet* side of the floor! Other happenings added to my frustration, and I fought my way out of a depressed mood. Satan was winning the battle, and I was sinking.

Thankfully Friday was much better. **I studied my Scripture cards and fought off the temptation to be mad.** I was jealous of my peers [for receiving what I had prayed for].

May 21, 2011

Two weeks ago I was assigned to Diane's team to work as a case advocate.

Last Friday, I met Derek for bowling [after receiving his call out of the blue]. We haven't been in touch since.

Last night, I met Wendy for dinner and a drink. She's doing well at her new job and still undecided about her church home.

June 13, 2011

Work's going well. I closed five cases last week, a personal best! I have some difficult cases in my queue now. I pray God gives me the words to speak the truth [to the customers], representing our client well.

Other news: the Dallas Mavericks won the National Championship; I searched airfares to Wales to visit my aunt and uncle; Henry [ex-boyfriend] is engaged!

June 27, 2011 [Promoted]

Today was my first day in the Inline Department, and my new boss is Suzanne.

Two weeks ago, the unit manager came to my desk. She said there's a need for more people in Inline, and my name had come up. They believe I'll do well as an Inliner [auditing cases before closing]. **I accepted the position, although I don't feel I possess enough experience or knowledge.** I knew God's hand was in this, because while she was speaking, I sensed, *This is God's will.* He gave me favor to be moved to Inline.

Thank you, Jesus, for this promotion and for walking ahead to clear the way! I will only succeed if you continue to guide me.

August 8, 2011 [Mental Attacks]

Inline is going well. I've completed 3 cases and no audits yet. I pray my first audit is a pass! God provided more coworkers to stop by my desk and say hello. It makes me feel visible and noticed and part of the group.

Much is stirring in my heart, and I can't describe it. I cried the past few times at church. I'm fighting a spirit of rejection. I ended my friendship with Derek for the second time, and I didn't handle it as well as I had hoped. **I should've prayed and waited on God, but I took matters into my own hands and made a mess.** I apologized later; yet I don't want to be his friend, the way he defines it. He wants to get to know me without dating, but isn't that the purpose?

Lord, please don't let me send another late-night, crazy email venting my emotions to a guy. I've done it to James, Henry, Mike, and now Derek. It doesn't encourage the receiver.

August 12, 2011

The last few days were challenging. They started well, but then something changed. Was it my thoughts or my hormones? **I felt like the Incredible Hulk one moment and on the verge of tears the next.** My acne was clearing up nicely until my period started.

A male coworker, a new friend from my team, underwent unexpected brain surgery. It was more involved than expected.

My trip to Wales is in two weeks!

August 23, 2011

At town hall it was announced that my coworker passed away from a brain infection, post-surgery. Several people gasped. My heart started pounding while I fought to suppress my natural instinct to cry. **For five hours, by the Lord's mighty hand, I kept my emotions stuffed down.** I started tearing up a few times at my desk. There's nothing like grieving the loss of a friend while being asked to continue working, surrounded by over two hundred people.

I pray for strength and comfort for his wife and family. I pray for strength and control of my emotions at work. Please fill me with your love and peace so I can be an example of stability for your glory. Cover me, Father. Restore me.

September 2, 2011 [First Trip to Wales]

I'm at DFW airport waiting for my flight to visit my aunt and uncle. My cousin is picking me up in London and driving me to Cardiff. I'm thankful for the opportunity to get to know Dad's side of the family and see England for the first time.

The past week at work was challenging, because my team lead said I need to work faster. Apparently, what I assumed a few weeks ago was true—I'm not up to speed like the other new people.☹ I was really sad, because I'm trying so hard. After our meeting, my confidence was shaken. I can't work faster, because I take longer to process information. **Only God can change me and how I think.**

September 3, 2011

It's almost 11:00 p.m. British Standard time.

On the flight, I sat next to a man from IBM who lectures at universities across the globe. He was dressed in a ball cap and jeans, and I secretly wondered if he was the CEO. A British flight attendant named John served our area. He was friendly and witty and enjoyed giving me a hard time. When I got off the plane, I waved and thanked him. He smiled and waved back, saying, "My pleasure" with that British accent.

September 4, 2011

Today is Sunday, 6:00 p.m. and it's drizzling outside. This morning I used all the hot water because I didn't know the shower water is separate from the tub water. I turned on the tub full blast and then turned on the shower! Oops! I won't do that again.

For breakfast, I had half a grapefruit and tea, with a croissant and homemade gooseberry jam! Then my cousin, uncle, and I drove to the wildlife reserve and saw dozens of geese, swans, and ducks. I took many nice pictures.

I presented my gifts last night. My aunt received a shawl, my uncle a leather toiletry bag, and my cousin a necklace. Dinner was trout, potatoes, green beans, peas, and carrots with a glass of Sauvignon Blanc. Dessert was a Christmas pudding made of raisins and dried fruits, stuck together with butter and beer, microwaved, topped with Cognac and lit with a match. We ate it with a scoop of vanilla custard.

September 5, 2011

Today is Monday, about 5:00 p.m. We had tea and cake in the front room, after driving to a "folly" (replica) of a medieval castle. The scenery was beautiful along the road through the woods—I expected to see Hansel and Gretel walk by!

We drove to a neighboring village to see a real castle, Caerphella, in the middle of town. My uncle planned to drive us along the bay, but his car overheated so we headed home. Tomorrow, we may ride the bus to the bay. We talked about touring Bath on Wednesday, a day predicted for sunny skies. Since the car is having issues, we may not go. Also, my uncle has been ill since my arrival. He has shingles along one side of his head and possibly into his eyelid.

I learned that my aunt and uncle are areligious, not practicing any religion. I thought they were Jewish. Their son is Jewish and takes his sons to synagogue. My cousin and her husband are also areligious.

I pray for health and healing of my uncle, his car, and for dry weather the rest of the week. I'm going downstairs now to join my family for television.

September 7, 2011

Yesterday my aunt and I went into town to see City Hall, Cardiff Art Museum, Sir David's Opera Hall, and the Law Courts. It was cold and windy, but no rain. We shopped at Marks & Spencer, where I bought two jackets and two sweaters. We went to John Lewis for a coffee break and then took the bus home. After dinner, we watched "World's Greatest Singer." This opera singing competition has aired for twenty-eight years in Cardiff. I picked the winner—Valentina from Moldova!

Today was colder and windier than yesterday. I don't desire to live here in the UK. The weather is too gray and wet. It's almost 5:30 p.m., and we'll be inside for another five to six hours, I suppose. We aren't going to Bath, and the sightseeing is almost over. It appears that I won't get to eat "fish and chips" before I leave.

September 9, 2011 [Severe Pain]

Today has been the longest day ever! I got up at 6:00 a.m. and arrived at the bus station in the rain. My "coach" left at 8:30 a.m. for London Heathrow. I ate lunch at a pub in the airport—fish and chips with peas. I chatted with the pub manager, a Korean man named Vinnie. He sat down with me and asked where I was from. He brought me a sample of English ale and a free cappuccino. He said Britain is best to visit in May to June.

Our flight takeoff was delayed forty-five minutes, and we made an emergency stop in Canada because two passengers needed medical attention. Eventually I felt faint and clammy. Was it anxiety? Claustrophobia? A nearby passenger switched seats so I would have space to lie down.

For the record, my symptoms are: congestion, sneezing, runny nose, constipation, and intense pain in my lower right back. The pain started mildly this morning and has dramatically increased. I can't relax because however I sit—leaning left, right, center, forward, or straight back—is excruciating. Maybe it's a pinched nerve or muscle spasm? All I know is that Advil isn't touching the pain.

I hope my painful back issues are gone when I wake up tomorrow. I may have to see a doctor. I want off this plane! I feel like I've been on here for days! Dear Jesus, heal me!

September 11, 2011

I finally made if off the dreadful twelve-hour flight.

When I woke up the next day, my pain was just as bad. I took 3 Advil and a hot shower. I iced my back for fifteen minutes every hour. It feels much better! Several friends on Facebook suggested a chiropractor.

I'm considering a visit to the dermatologist for my acne. It continues to get worse and it takes months for the scarring to fade.

November 4, 2011 [First Chiropractor]

Almost two months since my last entry. This is sad because so many good things have taken place that I may forget some!

My massage therapist massaged the knots out of my back. She gave me a bottle of acai juice that cleared my acne better than [the prescription medications].

That same week, I visited a friend's chiropractor. **Nervous and anxious, I read my Scripture cards while waiting in the office.** I told him that I'm afraid of being adjusted. I was scared, but knew God could heal me through Dr. Hooten. I felt a noticeable improvement the next day. After two more visits, I noticed less neck tension, and my back didn't hurt sitting at work! I'm 7 weeks into treatment and feel more relaxed and less anxious. My manager noticed after two weeks. I *felt* the difference, and others *saw* it in my face and body. Praise God!

Work is going well with thirteen [of my client audits] passing in a row! **God is faithful. I praise Him for guiding me through.** I also made friends with an unexpected person who has a reputation for being difficult to work with. We bonded over a big case and then made lunch plans to celebrate. I thank God for giving me the words to say, that she would come to like me.

My brother and nieces came up for my birthday. We had a fun time at dinner and church.

Last night, I had dinner with Clay for 3½ hours. He's competing in his 3rd Ironman race.

December 31, 2011 [Blue Christmas]

My entries lately have been very inconsistent. I used to write several times a week; I must make more of an effort to resume.

Christmas was spent without family, and I was disappointed my dinner plans were cancelled Friday night. I ate alone Saturday night after the Christmas Eve service because everyone scattered [to be with their families]. **Yes, I shed tears of loneliness and felt abandoned** by friends and family, *but* I'm grateful Mom and Dad hosted Renee's parents for Christmas dinner in Michigan.

Changes at work—big news! Our client project ends January 31 and the "ramp down" phase begins next week. The Inline department will be the last group to roll off. I plan to stick with CGC and see this through.

January 1, 2012

The start of the New Year has been rocky. In the past few weeks, 7 friends have let me down, some multiple times. . . .

I shall linger no longer on my disappointments; **I will pray for one female Christian friend who's reliable, dependable, and has similar interests.**

January 19, 2012 [First Layoff Experience]

The past 3 days have felt like a week, and I'm emotionally drained.

Human Resources terminated forty-eight people. They were told to collect their items, say goodbye, and leave the building. I got choked up hearing John pack because he really needed his job, worked lots of overtime, and was an excellent employee. I hugged him at the elevator and he wiped away one of my tears. I managed to whisper, "God bless you." Ken [coworker] walked me outside to clear my head. On the way, I saw Barret packing and hugged him goodbye. He has a newborn at home and a wife with severe back pain.

My employer released 25 percent of the staff, and I wasn't prepared. It was a long, awful day. Plus, I promised a friend (who had surgery) that I'd bring her dinner after work; I couldn't cancel on her but *really* wanted to be alone.

February 3, 2012 [Shared My Testimony]

At lunch on Tuesday, I shared my testimony with Ken. He converted to Catholicism after marrying his wife. It was a special time talking with a friend.

Our next work project is not yet ready, so we started doing community service. On Thursday, I volunteered at a resale shop and then met a coworker for dinner. He does not yet know Jesus as his personal Savior but he attends church. His heart and mind have not been transformed by His love; and for that reason, I cannot date him.

Yesterday eighty people were laid off, including several team leads. Two of my friends were released.

I recently accepted Thrive's social coordinator position, a one-year commitment. I think the experience will be good for me.

February 13, 2012 [Super Surprise]

I found out at the Super Bowl party that Mike and Sheryl are dating! At first I was hurt, a bit jealous, and insecure. The next day I realized that Satan had set the trap. I can *choose* how I will react moving forward, so I emailed Sheryl about having coffee—we meet in 3 days. **God gave me the idea to reach out to her in love in order to break off my selfishness.** I praise God, because it broke the wave of emotions!

Tomorrow is Valentine's Day. It's the *first* year that I can remember where I don't have a date and *I don't care*! Usually, I feel sorry for myself and jealous of those in relationships. My time will come. God is preparing The One He has chosen. I thank and praise Him for that!

February 20, 2012

It's 4:00 a.m. on Monday, and I can't fall back asleep! Last week I met Sheryl for tea. We chatted for two hours about our childhoods, families, and testimonies. Praise God!

Things have changed at work: ten people were selected for one bank project and five for another, leaving fifty-five of us waiting for an assignment. Ken left after accepting an offer with another company. I'll miss his friendship, especially with all the downtime we have now. I counted 7 lunch buddies now gone.

February 29, 2012 [3rd Round of Lay-offs]

Today is leap day! But I got laid off, with sixteen others. Some were assigned a new project, while the rest of us were sent home. I filed for unemployment after stopping at Marble Slab Creamery. I'm still in shock at the suddenness of today's events. CGC was generous to keep us on "the bench" for 3 weeks. New projects are a ways off, but we are eligible for rehire. **Meanwhile I'll spend time with God to learn what He wants me to do.** Thoughts of Dr. Leaf come to mind, as well as opening a tall women's clothing shop.

March 17, 2012

I've been unemployed for two weeks and two days. Love it!

I had 3 phone interviews with a large water treatment services company. I'm very interested in the company, but not the position.

March 28, 2012

I got a callback yesterday from CGC and met with the recruiter today at 3:00 p.m. They are hiring for a new project. My former team lead told me that I would do well as a QA reviewer and would like it *more* than my previous role!

April 5, 2012 [First Trip to Los Angeles]

I got back late Monday night from [visiting a church friend who moved to California]. She took me to the Chinese Theater and Hollywood Walk of Fame, where celebrities autographed their cemented handprints. We walked across the Sidewalk Stars and I saw Billy Graham's star. I returned home to discover termites in my kitchen counter. Ugh!

May 18, 2012

The Lord knows I have issues. I know it too. After feeling out of sorts—crying at Thrive when I shared my prayer request to be less selfish, critical, and judgmental—I spent time with God. **He restored me via His Word and through remembering who I am in Christ.**

I've done well all week, until tonight. It was Taste of Addison [and I got jealous when a guy I liked, and who I thought liked me, gave his full attention to my friend]. I felt excluded and abandoned. By the time he made an attempt to speak with me later that night, I was already feeling hurt and rejected. I know Satan is distorting truth to make me fall. I don't want to be jealous, hurt, or insecure.

May 20, 2012 [First Trip to Reno]

Doing better, praise God, since Taste of Addison! It wasn't anyone's fault, but my own insecurities and root of rejection.

Two weeks ago I was in Reno, Nevada, visiting Jim and Melisa. Jim and I had met in Italy on the Rick Steves tour in 2010. I gave him a Dallas book of sights and landmarks. For Melisa (not knowing her), I bought the book *Heaven Is for Real,* written by the little boy who [almost] died but came back to life after meeting Jesus and seeing heaven.

Clay and I plan to meet up in June. I'm still praying about him.

May 27, 2012 [Blessings]

Vicki, a team leader, requested that I be transferred to her team. I'm now on the customer servicing team, which is highly regarded by our client. I'm flattered and humbled.

Other news: I hosted a singles game night, where God gave me the grace to relax and enjoy the party with forty guests! I haven't hosted such a huge event since the Labor Day cookout in 2010. **It was evidence of growth and God's mighty grace working in me.**

Pat from work invited me to lunch. We talked about doing Celebrate Recovery together. I also considered Christian counseling, because even though I'm over the Taste of Addison event with my friend and that guy, it doesn't mean the *root* of insecurity is gone. It pops up from time to time. I want it gone, with the Lord's help!

My parents listed their house in Michigan for sale. [They are planning to downsize and finally move to Texas!]

June 9, 2012 [Mental Attacks]

I tried to calm down and trust God [during my first time-sensitive task on my new team]. I didn't feel that I was doing it right, and no one could help me. Thank God for an email from our client! She said we did an awesome job in such a short time. Praise Jesus! He was directing me the whole time my brain was full of fear.

Now I need to work on how I manage stress. I need the Lord's help. I think work-related tasks and relationships with coworkers are my biggest sources of anxiety—fear of failure, abandonment, and rejection. A church friend gave me the name of her counselor. **I'm aware that I have a root of rejection that leads to insecurity, anxiety, and jealousy (men/dating).**

I scheduled foundation repair for July 27.

It's also worth mentioning that Clay and I talked five and a half hours over sushi! [After much hesitation and prayer,] I mailed him a note regarding the possibility that *maybe* God's plan is for us to be together. I asked him to pray about it.

June 13, 2012

Work's going really well, but I haven't heard from Clay. Who knows if he opened my note? **I pray for God's will to be done and a prepared heart for the outcome.**

This is a year of engagements for people my age. If Clay doesn't see "us" as a possibility, I may rejoin eHarmony.

June 23, 2012 [My Office Ministry Begins]

Pat from work met me for church last week. Lucy, a new hire living in Lewisville, may join me this Sunday.

It's been almost been two weeks since I mailed the letter. I haven't heard from Clay. That can't be good. I hope he's sensitive to my position and will respond delicately. Should I continue waiting? Maybe he never got it?

July 7, 2012 [Slaying the Giant]

A lot has happened since my last entry. I sent Clay a text and he searched for my note in his pile of mail. He thanked me for writing and said he had wondered the same. We're meeting July 20 to discuss. Praise God, he's open to the idea! Clay has many qualities that I desire in a spouse.

Work got crazy. Vicki told me on Thursday at 3:30 p.m. that I'm being moved to a *new* project, I'm joining a new group of testers, and she is no longer my team lead. She said all this right before leaving on vacation. Also, I will show [our client vice president] my testing steps via teleconference next week!

I needed to become more familiar with the test. I spent twelve and a half hours on my PowerPoint before the client modified the spreadsheet [which meant that I had to change my presentation at the last minute]. Let's just say that I battled fear and anxiety, being thrust into a new role with little support. **God carried me through, and the presentation went better than expected.**

It was my toughest week at CGC and I was *desperate* for Jesus! I faced my Goliath, and the enemy was all over me. I recited Scriptures out loud—Isaiah 26:3, 2 Timothy 1:7, and Isaiah 41:10 and 40:31. I read the story of David and Goliath repeatedly. My favorite parts:

1. David shouted to Goliath, "You come to me with sword, spear, and javelin, but I come to you in the name of the LORD Almighty" (1 Samuel 17:45 NLT).

2. Verse 48: "As Goliath moved closer to attack, David quickly ran out to meet him." David ran *toward* Goliath with the *assurance* that the Lord Almighty was on his side. I love that!

In my work situation, I was thrown into a "battle." With no weapon of choice, no armor, no cheering squad, I made up my mind that I was going to move forward. **Jesus was by my side as I carried my cross each day. He was my *only* comfort.**

July 20, 2012 [The Answer]

Wow, I'm in shock. The night did not go as I expected, as I hoped. Clay has been dating someone casually for 3 months and hasn't felt an indication from God that he should date me, although there were moments in the past when he thought about it.

God never promised it would turn out the way I envisioned. I just wasn't prepared for Clay's words. I feel a rush of emotions with an overall numbness. I'm hurt, angry, confused, and disappointed. I trusted that I did what God led me to do by writing the note. Help me, Jesus!

July 25, 2012

Maybe I was selfish to think Clay would drop her and date me. I pray again for God's will to be done and for the grace to accept it. **I've obeyed God, and now I need to let it go and get it off my mind.** I'm praying about eHarmony again.

August 12, 2012

Foundation repair is done, $4,500 later. Nine piers have lifted the front of my house.

Mom and Dad closed on their new house in San Antonio on July 27.

Work's going well. God blessed me with rapport with my new teammates and a relaxed attitude that only comes from Him. Satan still attacks and wants me to worry and be anxious.

September 14, 2012

My period is in progress, and I have been able to feel my patience decreasing since Wednesday. Being off the prescribed acne meds, my hormones are more intense. I pray God will teach me how to work through this without my emotions taking over.

October 14, 2012 [Sharing My Testimony to a Group]

On September 30, I shared my testimony at Thrive. God spoke though me; I was on autopilot! I read my story, 3 pages, without crying; this was my prayer (in addition to not being afraid). I felt *amazing* when I finished; I'm grateful for trusting God to do it! I was on a high for days. There was more I wanted to say, but I trust that whatever I shared was what God wanted me to say. I believe He used my story to touch others, each in a unique way. **God does powerful things through our testimony when we are willing to be vulnerable and share it openly.**

I cried today during the service. Perhaps I'm transitioning after my parents visit, adjusting to being alone again. It's nice to have their help with the challenges of homeownership. I'm praying for God to restore my mind, mood, and attitude. I miss my quiet time with Him.

December 30, 2012 [Mailing My Testimony]

The past two months have been a blur.

I went to work Friday, when 25 percent of our workforce was laid off. Lucy's safe. [She's a new coworker friend who has attended church with me.]

Derek asked me out again and I declined. God had answered my prayer to reveal his heart. My gut was correct— I'm on a different path, moving at a faster pace toward Jesus.

I've heard nothing from Clay, although I mailed him a Christmas card with my printed testimony. I enclosed a copy to all my friends and family who received Christmas cards.

January 1, 2013

Happy New Year! I'm on the sofa with a blanket, enjoying a fire. Usually I'm energized at a New Year's beginning, excited for changes and answered prayers ahead. This year I feel more melancholy. The cold weather and cloudy skies aren't helping, and neither are my hormones. I've gone six months without the acne meds due to lawsuits and health warnings.

Our desks at work moved from the quiet, private corner to the main area. We're in the open, exposed like sitting ducks. Being tall, my head is above the cube walls and visible from every direction. It'll take some getting used to.

Pete stopped by and said hello. It was our first conversation since the company Christmas party. Am I wrong to think he may be interested? He's a Christian and a friend of Lucy.

January 11, 2013

My acne has flared up the worst in months—face, neck, and back. Please, Lord, cure me of this curse!

I'm also struggling with my attitude and hormones. I'm feeling down [about an interaction with a male coworker]. **Dear Lord, help me to forgive myself** and allow me to lay this down at your feet. I need to let go of my grip. Renew my mind, Lord, and fill me with your truth, love and peace.

January 22, 2013 [Mental Attacks]

Four days of consistent flirting—I prayed and asked God if Pete knew Him. I came to work eager to talk to him, but all morning passed and nothing. I decided to instant message him in the afternoon, and our conversation was flat. About this time, Satan jumped in my mind, filling me with lies, but I didn't recognize it! I got hurt and then mad at Pete. Later I repented for getting frustrated and reaching out to him. I apologized to God for not trusting Him. I don't want things to be awkward.

Lord, restore me. I love you, Jesus.

February 14, 2013

Lucy invited Pete to my house on the 23rd for sushi-making. It was *her* idea to invite him. She wrote over instant messaging, "Pete's coming too. Oh, and I may be wrong, but I think he may like you."

February 23, 2013 [No Sushi for You!]

Lucy came over, but Pete didn't. At the last minute, he went out with his roommate! He had told me that he was looking forward to making sushi. Yesterday he looked me in the eye and said it again as we walked out of work together. I asked Lucy if Pete was a player. She paused, and I didn't get a straight answer.

Earlier I had prayed for God to show me the truth about Pete. Not only did he not show up, but Lucy cast him in a different light. Once again I'm deceived, hurt, and somewhat angry.

Lord, help me and forgive me! I played the fool again. What's my problem? Why can't I let it go and lay it down at the foot of the cross?

March 8, 2013 [Personal Revelation]

Thank you, Lord, for opening my eyes to see myself more clearly. **I have a deep wound from a root of rejection that started in childhood. It grew in my adult years and is the basis for my insecurity, anxiety, fear, shame, anger, and control issues that rise up from time to time.** I'm able to understand this, because God has walked me through the past sixty days regarding *my actions* and *reactions* toward Pete. I was up and down and all over the board. I felt happy and secure, and then rejected and down, with this taking place in my mind.

Joyce Meyer says our soul is our carnal nature—what we think, what we want, and what we feel. My carnal nature has thrown fits over [guys], even though my mind knows it's foolish. It's a waste of emotional energy and time.

I realized that I often "feel" rejected by someone of the opposite sex, even though he may not be rejecting me. My reaction is to pull away, avoid, and pray that he'll go away. In the case of Pete, he's still there smiling and being friendly. God is teaching me how to be friends with him. My guard is up, and I keep my distance.

God is working in me and I feel more at peace. It'll take time for the full root of rejection to heal and be replaced with God's love. **This is why I've felt the "tug" the past few months; God has been moving me toward healing and restoration.** The Holy Spirit nudged me toward a break from Thrive, and I attended a women's retreat, "Unmasked: Free to Be Me," which the Lord put on a friend's heart to invite me to. I see now how all the parts fit together—the desire to break from Thrive, the turmoil with Pete and my expectations, and my intense desire to spend more time with the Lord. This feels good; I'm on the right path, and God is with me.

I skipped service last Sunday and stayed home to pray and reflect on my notes from the retreat. I've developed certain actions and behaviors to cope with my wounds—fear, shame, anger, anxiety, and control. They all trace back to the root of rejection. I need to develop new actions and reactions, with God's help.

April 1, 2013 [Healing Journey Begins]

I'm sitting on my patio watching the sunset. It's still and peaceful.

I started the Candida diet; the first week was rough, missing two days of work and sleeping a lot. This is week two of not eating gluten, sugar, starches, dairy, almonds, fruit, vinegar, salad dressings, and eggs.

I enjoy not having Thrive. I feel free from all the emails, activities, and events. This peace is confirmation that I am being obedient.

I'm taking new supplements, per the wellness doctor. I feel great and sleep deeper.

God still has work to do in my mind. Renee sent me Joyce Meyer's *Developing Power Thoughts* package that includes a study guide. Tonight was my first night. The first Power Thought is based on Philippians 4:13: "I can do whatever I need to do in life through Christ."

As much as I didn't want to, I had made Pete an idol. **Satan used him as a distraction, but God is using him to teach me the truth about myself.** It's been a bumpy ride. My job is to lay it all down, and Satan is putting up a fight. I continue praying for healing and courage to trust God with my heart and relationships.

May 3, 2013

Tonight my phones are off; I'm exhausted.

Rachel [from high school] flew in this week to see her father in the Fort Worth hospital. We had a wonderful dinner on the rooftop of the Reata. The last time we met was 3 years ago in Michigan [when she begged me to join Facebook and I gave in].

My team was recognized at town hall for our hard work and adaptability. God had guided me through an [urgent and lengthy] task assisting with screen shots. Little did I know that I would be trained as the primary tester! It's been confusing and stressful, but I felt led to step up—an opportunity to trust God. **I needed Jesus desperately, as I was mentally, physically, and emotionally stretched beyond my limits.**

October 20, 2013 [First Holy Spirit Call Out]

I turned thirty-seven and received many cards this year. As loved as I feel on my birthdays, though, there's an evil spirit that wars in my mind, tempting me to be disappointed with my singleness and how my life has turned out. I haven't melted down in months, and God has done amazing things in me and through me since March 2013: Candida diet; the start of physical healing of acne, anxiety, and allergies; *and* spiritual healing of self-pity, discontentment, and unforgiveness. I'm still renewing my mind.

I went to a women's dream workshop at Covenant Church where the ladies prayed over me to release a spirit of shame and for protection from lies in my mind. [*] I cried after one of the speakers [had looked around the room, pointed to me in the back, and] said that I "stuff things down" and I'm "on the edge of transition." Both are true.

[*I didn't know the ladies at the workshop; the Holy Spirit had revealed truths about me to the speaker. Right before she pointed at me, I heard the Holy Spirit whisper, "Hold on!"]

I signed up for IBC small groups and look forward to starting in January 2014.

Today I volunteered in the church nursery—two hours of crying off and on. I was disappointed that I didn't love it. After praying and waiting six months, I had hoped the nursery would prepare me for motherhood, but the chaos (feeding times, kids' allergies, diapers, and paperwork) made my head spin. So I'm praying for clarity.

Roofers and contractors came out to inspect my interior wall cracks. More foundation shifting!

October 21, 2013 [More Layoffs]

Many friends at work have resigned. CGC also had 3 rounds of layoffs.

As far as IBC, I think the children's ministry is not where I belong. When I think of my passions—nutrition, health, and wellness—they deal with adults.

Clay was laid off 3 weeks ago. I gave him a book by Jack Graham, *Man of God*. I pray the Holy Spirit uses it as a catalyst for spiritual growth during his season of self-reflection.

November 2, 2013

Clay and I had a nice lunch after church. We talked until 3:30 p.m. He suggested meeting before his Ironman on the 17th. So I wait and pray.

November 16, 2013

I went to the zoo with my neighbor Dana and her girls last Sunday. I had prayed with Dana and then let her sleep while she iced her back. I had skipped church to play with the girls, and she really appreciated my help. I know God has me here to assist her. We are meeting at IBC tomorrow for the service.

Clay met me at Pei Wei on my lunch break. He bought my meal and gave me a birthday card with a fifty-dollar gift card!

I feel peace in my heart regarding where I am in life. Peace in my friendships, peace at work, and peace with Clay. I'm learning to "let go" and "let God" lead me. I'm blessed and thankful.

December 7, 2013

Clay and I met for dinner before Thanksgiving and he paid for the 3rd time in a row. We haven't talked about dating, but it seems to be headed that way. Now that I have a smartphone, we've been texting more.

December 17, 2013

The CGC holiday party was at the Frontiers of Flight Museum in Dallas, and Clay was my guest. **It feels like we're dating, but there's still a distance between us.** We don't talk on the phone, but he texts daily.

My thoughts need to be on Jesus and eternal things. "Fix your thoughts on what is true and honorable and right. Think about things that are pure and lovely and admirable" (Philippians 4:8 NLT).

December 28, 2013

I was in San Antonio over Christmas. I greatly enjoyed myself (praise the Lord!) because of one-on-one time with Mom at Starbucks, sushi with my brother, and watching *The Nutcracker* with Dad. One night the whole family came over, another we took my nieces out for dinner, and another night my parents and I dined out. It was a nice mix of events. My sister-in-law, nieces, mother, and I attended a Christmas Eve service.

I had lunch today with Lucy. She's getting baptized on February 23 and will join Irving Bible Church as a member! I'm proud of her! I mailed her a Christmas card with 3 gift cards. She loved it.

Two weeks ago, I met Jasmine [church friend] for dinner and service at The Village Church.

Dana and family may go to church with me tomorrow, another friend wants to get together, and Renee called early this morning. **Many people are reaching out to me, and it can feel overwhelming when I desire to spend more time**

alone with God. Even now, I planned to have quiet time to read and pray, but I'm writing instead.

December 31, 2013 [Mental Attacks]

It's New Year's Eve and I'm staying in. Dana invited me over, but I'm too tired.

I thought Clay would respond to my messages when he returned from California. Today is NYE, and he didn't mention getting together. It turned out that he didn't receive my last 3 texts, and that's why I didn't hear back. The enemy had me considering: (1) he forgot to respond; (2) he chose not to respond; (3) he met someone he wants to date; or (4) he's too busy to respond. All were lies, and I recognized it as another attack; however, the crazy lies got louder and I got upset. I was tempted to feel sorry for myself; but I gave up self-pity earlier this year, so this was the first time it showed up knocking at my door.

Satan knows my fear of rejection, especially in dating relationships. **I see now how he has injected lies into my mind that have caused me to behave or react emotionally to misunderstandings.** Just like in the workplace, Satan sets me up to get me upset or insecure.

January 3, 2014 [New Crush]

There's a guy at work who seems really sweet, but I don't know if he's a Christ follower. I said a prayer yesterday that I would see him today, and we walked in from the parking garage together. His name is Jim. I sense that he's interested in me; but if he's not a believer, there's no point.

January 17, 2014

I think this will be a great new chapter in my life! I really connected with my IBC small group leaders and will meet the rest of the group soon.

Tierny [coworker] is coming over for dinner. I'm cooking salmon, rice, and veggies.

January 22, 2014

3:15 a.m.

Small group was interesting. I liked the people but had concerns about the format. I considered changing groups or hosting my own gathering. Is that where the Lord is leading? Or am I to stay, even though I may not grow in my understanding and application of the Bible?

Lucy will give her video testimony for baptism this Sunday. I offered to pick her up, take her to service and lunch, and then stay for her session. Altogether, that's four hours. *The Purpose Driven Life* **says love is spelled T-I-M-E.** There's no greater way to show love for others than to spend (or sacrifice) your time with them.

God is stretching and growing me in my current relationships. I question my need to belong to a small group because I have people to "do life with." I help my neighbor and reach out to new people at the office. I'm not without flaws, but I am aware of the people around me.

I had lunch with Clay but haven't done a "heart check." I'm no longer satisfied hanging out. I want him to pursue me in a dating relationship. Renee has urged me to do this, and the Holy Spirit may be prompting. **My desire to be pursued is healthy—that's how God made women.** I don't want to pressure him, but I can't stay in this gray area, anticipating and hoping his heart will turn. Like James, Clay's not on fire for me.

January 26, 2014 [Another Crossroad]

As suspected, he's not ready to move forward. We discussed expectations, but there was no clear resolution. I'm seeking wisdom if Clay asks to meet again. Do I decline? Do I accept but join eHarmony so I can explore other avenues? What would Dr. Phil say? What would Jesus say?

Meanwhile I find myself drawn to Jim at work. I was walking down the hallway and heard a faint, "Charlotte." I turned around and it was Jim! I smiled and said hello. He said, "I just wanted to say hi." Is he a believer, Lord? I wish he would ask me to lunch so I can assess his spiritual position, especially since Clay is on the fence.

February 23, 2014

A month has passed, and there's much to share:
- Clay and I agreed to date slowly, letting things unfold.
- Lucy was baptized at IBC today! I sat with her in the second row. She did the verse reading before the sermon and was featured in the baptism video. I'm so proud of her for facing her fears and doing it! I gave her a *Jesus Calling* devotional and a leather bracelet.
- Renee was matched by a friend to a wonderful guy named Steve. He seems to be a solid Christian man who adores her. I hope this is The One God has sent!
- Nisa gave birth to baby James, their second child.
- Small group didn't work out. I'm considering a friend's referral about a ladies Bible study in my area that claims to be serious about Jesus.

February 28, 2014

Last night, I got frustrated with Clay for not making plans to get together, and taking twelve hours to respond to my text from lunchtime! He apologized, and yet when I replied to him at 3:30 p.m. today, it's 8:00 p.m. and nothing. I'm tempted to get upset with him for making me feel like I'm on a waiting list to get his attention. I am setting him free!

I will reactivate eHarmony to use the rest of my 3-month membership.

Lord, help me to *hear* your voice and walk in your ways! I need *you* to guide me and renew my mind.

March 1, 2014

 Clay responded that he's fine with a break. I wrote back saying that I respect, admire, and care for him. I thanked him for his kindness and friendship and apologized that I can no longer wait. Five hours later (LOL), he wrote back saying that he respects me and understands. I am sad that we are not in the same place.

 Tierny [coworker] is coming over at 6:00 p.m. for sushi and a movie.

 I woke up today at 4:30 a.m. without my alarm and spent two hours reading, praying, and meditating on Scripture: "Let us strip off every weight that slows us down, especially the sin that so easily hinders our progress. And let us run with endurance the race that God has set before us. We do this by keeping our eyes on Jesus, on whom our faith depends from start to finish" (Hebrews 12:1-2 NLT).

March 2, 2014 [Accepting God's Will]

 My moods are up and down, but I know it's temporary. Four years of prayer that Clay may be The One has been answered: "No." I accept God's will and trust Him too much to feel sorry for myself. There is pain of disappointment, but that will fade.

 Two Christian coworkers are leaving, plus ten others are leaving the company. I feel low morale in my heart. I'm thankful [a particular coworker] is still here but we don't talk much lately. She lives her life on social media and I desire to seek God. We have different priorities. **The closer I get to Jesus, the wider the gap between people and me.**

 "So do not throw away this confident trust in the Lord. Remember the great reward it brings you! Patient endurance is what you need now, so that you will continue to do God's will. Then you will receive all that he has promised" (Hebrews 10:35, 36 NLT).

March 4, 2014

I registered for the Dr. Leaf conference in August. Jasmine and my hair stylist are both interested but can't commit. I had dinner with Jasmine last Sunday, and she came over Monday to watch Dr. Leaf's 3rd DVD. She stayed two hours; it was so nice to spend time with her!

I started my tax return and spent time with the Lord. It's been a long and quiet weekend, which is how God wanted it to be. I haven't cried or felt sorry for myself regarding Clay.

Ash Wednesday is tomorrow. I plan to attend the IBC service with Jasmine. I'm eager to join a small group and find an additional place to serve at church or in the community. Possibly tutor chemistry students?

March 13, 2014 [Wedding Bells]

I called Renee and got the latest. She and Steve plan to marry by the end of this year! I'm happy for them!

An IBC staff member said there's a ministry of teachers tutoring disadvantaged students on Wednesdays. She will find out details and let me know.

March 30, 2014

Funny how fast things change. Renee and Steve are engaged to be married on May 31, and two guys from eHarmony are interested in meeting me.

Dad has been in the hospital since Thursday. He has atrial fibrillation (irregular heart beat) and retained water in his heart and lungs—congestive heart failure. Pneumonia and stroke are a risk, and his cardiologist recommends a strong drug to rid his body of excess water. He will be monitored more closely for side effects.

April 10, 2014

I'm enjoying the warm breeze and sunset from my patio. I met a guy from eHarmony on Sunday. He opened the restaurant door as I approached in the rain and presented me with a bouquet of lavender daisies! We will meet again, but I question the chemistry.

I'm also in communication with two guys named Tim. One is the "Houston Hottie" who appears to be sold-out on Jesus. The other is a business owner and father in New Mexico. He has an impressive profile as well—strong leader, creative, and hardworking. I have a strong desire to be his wife. I'm waiting on his reply after answering his questions. I shared that I've grown a lot in the past year and communicate with God regularly. He sends me people who need help, and I have a heart for those who are different and/or rejected by society. **I was very open and pray that he will not reject me.**

I'm taking a summer Bible study with Lucy. It's about God's grace, our thankfulness, and counting one hundred blessings.

April 13, 2014 [Door Closed]

Tim from New Mexico responded; but when I clicked to read his email, his profile was gone! He closed me out and I'll never know what he said. I was shocked. Once again, I got my heart involved too soon; the lies I believed have been exposed.

Please heal my wounded heart, Lord. I love you and trust you with all that I am. Protect my heart from further damage over the next few months.

April 23, 2014

I'm now in open communication with Tim in Houston and a pastor in California. I have 7 days left on eHarmony.

I went to church to begin tutoring high school students, but tutorials were cancelled. I stayed 30 minutes while an IBC staff member showed me around the youth area.

April 25, 2014

Another beautiful spring day! A bird is singing in my pear tree, and a breeze is rustling the leaves.

I have no plans tonight and sense an ache in my heart. Maybe God is pruning off one or both of my eHarmony matches? The pastor writes once a week. I responded on Tuesday and haven't heard back.

I'm thankful Jasmine is free for lunch tomorrow, since I'm feeling a bit sad. It may be hormones or God doing something in me.

I watched Tim's favorite sermon and there were *numerous* false teachings. I was horrified. If he writes back, I must tell him what I found. I pray his heart and eyes will be opened to the truth.

May 1, 2014 [Closing the Door]

I closed my eHarmony account last night. The experience was an emotional roller coaster. The time spent per week reading and responding plus the emotional impact was a waste of time! **Here I am ninety days later with no boyfriend, no dates, and wounds in my heart**. If I had invested those hours and thoughts into reading and reflecting on God's Word, I would have been better off.

I went to IBC yesterday to tutor. It was cancelled again, but no one notified me. I sat in the room for 30 minutes feeling anxious and forgotten.

As far as Tim, he wrote a long response quoting Scripture. His tone started neutral but then turned condescending. He said that talking to me was like talking to a second grader—I'm "too spiritually immature to understand the steak of the Word." He threw in some more jabs and then closed with "Blessings☺, Tim." My heart sank. I was hurt and offended. I responded:

> "Hi, Brother Tim. I wrote my email out of genuine concern for you. You could have left off the insults, but I understand where your loyalties lie. I will continue praying for you."

I referenced Colossians 3:12-14 about clothing ourselves in tenderhearted mercy, patience, peace, and forgiving others' faults. I ended:

> "We will continue this conversation in heaven.☺ Charlotte."

He wrote back fifteen minutes later:

> "Hey Sis. Sorry that you took offense to my remarks. I probably could have worded them with more grace. I wanted to get your attention—to wake you up. I hope you will take a look at the Scriptures I gave you."

That's how my saga on eHarmony ended. The experience was draining and disappointing; however, God used me to plant seeds; John [*] was easy, Tim was difficult. One built me up in my faith, the other tore me down. To God be the glory.

[*I had one date with John where I delivered a message from the Lord. The Holy Spirit spoke through me, sharing lessons that God had recently taught me.]

I am a servant of the Lord Jesus Christ. Not everything He asks me to do will feel good. **I won't do everything right, but God will use my best attempts to accomplish His purpose.** I pray for Tim's eyes to be opened and for me to release any hurt or anger. I did my best to speak the truth in love.

May 2, 2014 [Journaling toward Jesus]

My life's speed has slowed down from one hundred to ten miles per hour! I am adjusting. This season I will return to a closer relationship with the Lord. I have read in Matthew [in the Bible] the past few nights and journaled too. I am more present in the moment but know that I have wounds from online dating.

I've grieved the Holy Spirit by refusing to follow His promptings this week: "Say hello," "Hold the elevator," "Turn around." Instead, I turned inward and licked my wounds of rejection. As a result, I've had a bad attitude at work and toward others.

May 28, 2014

The symphony was grand! Our seats were in the Choral Terrace. It was a visual delight, but not as acoustically pleasing as the Dress Circle where we sat for *Beethoven's Ninth* (Lucy's first symphony).

My parents arrived last Thursday. We went to the 5:00 p.m. service and sat with Lucy, who read the Scripture on stage. Pastor Andy spoke about pride versus humility; ironically, Dad is prideful and Mom is humble. **I'm so glad that Dad's heart is opening to the truth of God, and that he attends church with me.** [Answered prayer!]

Work has slowed down, I'm not dating anyone, and my attraction to Jim grows.

June 7, 2014

Last weekend was Renee's wedding in Raleigh. It was surreal being there with her family and meeting Steve and his family. I stepped into her world and felt out of touch with what her life has become.

June 15, 2014

The past week was a bit up and down spiritually/emotionally. My flesh flared up 3 times; it may have been a test. My focus shifted from God and others to my own desires. I'm praying to fix my thoughts on things that are pure, lovely, admirable, true, honorable, and right (Philippians 4:6-8).

I realized my unhealthy thought process regarding men I'm attracted to is harmful to my well-being. I am a child of the King and a pearl of great price! **These fantasies and "false truths" are not leading me toward peace or joy or to Jesus.** They pull me toward the world—overeating, drinking, lust, etc. I pray the Lord will reprogram my brain so I can change this pattern.

I'm excited about Dr. Leaf's conference in August. Jasmine said she'll join me but hasn't registered yet.

A friend and I hit Sprinkles for dessert. Two other
Charlotte's were there—one older and one younger! We all
spell it the same and were named after someone in our family.
Amazing, 3 Charlotte's in Sprinkles at the same time!

June 21, 2014

Today is my spiritual birthday! I was baptized eleven years
ago at Fellowship Church after accepting Jesus as my Lord
and Savior the previous summer. God has grown me and
healed me so much in the past few years! As a result, I
struggle with pride.

I've prayed for weeks for God to remove my desire to date
Jim, to renew my mind, and to redirect my thoughts. This
saga is another test. I struggle with false beliefs and raised
expectations; I learned this last year with Pete. **I take facts
and "fill in the blanks" with my ideas and reasoning, and
then believe them as truth.**

If I step *way* back and think about it, there's nothing I can
do to change God's will. I'm learning to trust God and die to
self. It's *hard*! I've resorted to overeating and some whiskey,
and I confess this lust as *sin*! I am weak, but I know the Lord
is doing a good work in me. It hurts like hell, but in the end, it
will be worth it!

June 29, 2014

I prayed for God to remove my pride and lust; the lust has
subsided and my pride was humbled. **I'm under construction
and the Holy Spirit is tearing down walls.** I *know* the
finished product will be awesome! The stronghold is coming
down. Thank you, Jesus!

July 11, 2014 [Mental Attacks]

I'm outside enjoying the evening. My parents and brother
were here and we watched the final episode of *Touched by an
Angel*. The DVD set was a Christmas gift from Mom.

Danny [welding friend] and I talked for 3 hours over dinner. I told him about my food allergies, physical healing, spiritual healing of self-pity, and learning to love others. It was great to share it all! **God has done so much the past sixteen months, I feel like a different person.** I'm the healthiest I've ever been—body, mind, and spirit.

However, the enemy attacked me heavily before, during, and after our new client manager came to the office. I haven't been that bombarded with fear, lies, and worry in a long time. My spiritual tank was on "E" because of my parent's visit. Next time, I should get up earlier, even fifteen minutes, to read in my Bible and pray each morning. I need God *every* hour of *every* day!

Regarding Jim, I'm friendly but keeping distance.

Lord, help me hold out for my godly man of integrity! Society teaches men to "take charge" and be "in control" of their careers and destiny. I once lived that way. I'm grateful Jesus is steering my ship, because He knows where I need to be!

July 13, 2014

I'm on my patio in the stillness of morning. It's cool and restful, with birds chirping and planes flying overhead. I am grateful for God's blessings.

Life often pulls us forward at an unbearable pace, but I refuse to get pulled under. Last week I burned out. I'm recovering with time in the Word, prayer, and journaling.

July 16, 2014 [Taking Action]

I did two bold things today and only regret one of them: (1) I sent Jim an email asking if he wanted to join me for lunch tomorrow. About 3 hours later, I saw him eating alone in the breakroom; (2) I walked over and sat down. He said he got my email but didn't read it.

Despite his kindness and flirty waving in the halls, he's not interested in getting to know me. Just like Pete, he's only playing. It hurts a little, but I've received freedom from the lies in my mind. It is an answered prayer—God says "no" again. **Like a child, sometimes we keep testing the boundaries to see if "no" is still "no" as time goes by.**

July 17, 2014 [More Attacks]

The enemy is flooding my mind with lies and excuses. Jim never responded to my invite. Here's the curve ball: at the end of the day, he waved, stopped to chitchat wearing a big smile, and then wished me a great weekend. *What is that*?!? Jim flirted as before, and yet ignored my email. I'm praying for him. He wants to flirt but not be my friend? No, thank you! Bait and switch—that's manipulative. I regret emailing him, because the enemy has pounced all day.

July 20, 2014 [Eyes Opened]

I am humbled. The events of the past week reflect that I'm not as wise and discerning as I thought. I was fooled by reading too much into the actions of another and was impatient by taking things into my own hands. Life is about learning from our mistakes, and I've learned a lot. I pray that I don't repeat these in the future.

July 23, 2014 [Turning to Jesus]

I'm weary of getting attention from guys I don't want to date. I want to shout from a mountain top: "Please stop! Thank you, but no. Where is my Romeo? Where is my godly man of integrity? One who is wise and prepared for marriage? One who will treasure me as a woman of noble character, more precious than rubies? One who will cover me, provide for me, and guide me on the path the Lord has prepared for us. Where is he???"

[A certain coworker] is an example of a friend who disappoints me over and over. She's just too busy to text or email. Sorry, I'm venting my thoughts on everything now. . . I sometimes feel like my family doesn't know or understand me. Warren and Danny are my Christian father-figures who are busy with their own families, jobs, and churches. To recap: my friends, family, and coworkers are great people who are unable to meet my needs. **Therefore, I must turn to Jesus to become my healer, my love, my father and mother, my brother, and my friend.**

My Holy Spirit "flow" has been off. It makes sense that Satan would use Jim as a distraction, since my ministry is my workplace. If I'm focused on him, then I won't be serving the people God wants me to reach. Therein lies the battle; I want to love my coworkers but avoid Jim. Good thing the Dr. Leaf conference is next month—I need help!

A great quote from *Did I Kiss Marriage Goodbye,* attributed to Paul David Tripp[2]: "There is a direct relationship between expectation and disappointment. Most of the time in relationships people have not actually wronged us, but they have failed to meet our expectations."

July 26, 2014

Living for God and growing in knowledge and understanding have given me passion and purpose. You can tell someone what God showed you or what He did through you; but until *they* hunger and *seek* after Jesus, their life remains unchanged. I was once stagnant, but something changed when I left teaching. On a leap of faith, I trusted God to provide and He did. [I was led to CGC, where] He showed me that I didn't love my coworkers. Then my wellness journey began with Dr. Hooten at Maximized Living, Dr. Rector and the Candida diet, and Dr. Leaf and the renewing of my mind. I prayed with my parents for Dad's healing [for the first time]. God gave me favor at work and a greater leading and awareness of the Holy Spirit. I've matured, and yet pride, lust, anxiety, and fear still threaten my walk with Jesus.

The Purpose Driven Life has sharpened my focus, and I expect tutoring and the Jen Wilkin Bible study to be a fresh surge of growth. I feel like I have been in a waiting pattern for months.

July 31, 2014

It was a coworker's last day at the office. I'm grateful the Holy Spirit prompted me to recognize him at his last team huddle. Before I knew what I was doing, I was speaking—totally the Holy Spirit. He gave me the words to say, and my coworker was blessed.

I had dinner with Jasmine and told her about IBC's sermon and how I lack deep, spiritually mature friendships. Pastor Jay asked us to write down our closest friends and I wrote: Renee and Jasmine. I'm lacking friends who have more experience with the Lord than I do. Jasmine is wise but very busy with work, her grown daughter, and traveling. She knows that I need more from our friendship and offered to meet every Monday for dinner. I'm grateful she wants to move forward.

August 4, 2014 [Stood Up]

I'm at Thai Ruby alone; Jasmine just cancelled. I *knew* this would happen because she's never certain if she'll work late or get called in. The Holy Spirit prepared me an hour ago that she may cancel. I'm disappointed, but at least I will enjoy the red curry and serene surroundings.

Since Friday I've been out of sorts because of friendships. I posted on Facebook and some misunderstood my intentions and took it personally. Argh! I cleared it up with the 3 friends who commented, but who knows how many others read it, took offense, and didn't say anything. The enemy has attacked me continuously since then.

August 7, 2014 [Fasting from Facebook]

I'm giving up Facebook to seek the Lord. **God is pruning me from the inside; it feels like a chainsaw, buzzing down everything at once.** Even Jasmine is being cut off. Maybe not permanently, but I sense that God is burning it all down to rebuild something else.

Yesterday was a hard day; everyone has been a disappointment. I've let it all go and will wait to see what God does and where He moves me. People don't understand, and that's why I need to reach out to Jesus and not people. The pain is temporary and for His glory.

I'm waiting to hear back from IBC regarding [my request for] a mentor.

There seems to be a strange combination of sadness, pain, and anger mixed in my spirit. I find myself annoyed at the world and worldly people. I want [true sisters] who seek after the Lord with all their heart and who have time to be a committed friend. Just one or two would be great.

I heard Dr. Tony Evans' radio broadcast on praise, *sacrifice*, and prayer while parked at Walmart. It was perfect timing! **The message confirmed my desire to fast, in order to hear from the Lord more clearly.** I've been praising Him through worship music all week. My current favorite song is "Hope in Front of Me" by Danny Gokey.

August 10, 2014 [Altar of Stones]

I spent part of yesterday in prayer, reading the Bible, and waiting on God. **I sat in silence thinking, waiting, talking to Him about what He's preparing me for.** He has quieted *all* of my friends except Renee, who is faithful to text daily. She knows I'm hurting and that God is pruning off many friendships.

After spin class I had a nice talk with Dong. His mom [from Vietnam] asked if she could sit with him the next time he prayed before bed. I pray that God will direct his words and open his mother's heart [to Jesus]. I asked him to pray for a godly mentor for me, one who is a wife and mother.

The enemy has been attacking me this week, especially the past few days. I've found it difficult to smile at people at work and haven't engaged in much conversation. I'm on a break from Facebook and from contacting friends. **I sense the Lord is asking me to not text, call, or email.** I may respond if they reach out to me, but I'm *not* to solicit conversation or social plans.

I'm thankful for my beautiful backyard. The peace and serenity that I experience at home is such a gift from God! It recharges my spirit. When I'm out here, the world stops and nature serenades me.

I selected four small stones from my garage. Using a Sharpie, I wrote "Marriage," "Mentor," "Ministry," and "True Friends"— one per stone. They are desires of my heart that I give to God daily. I placed them on the floor, symbolizing that they lay at the feet of Jesus. (A dove just landed on my roof. Doves remind me of the Holy Spirit. The Bible says in Matthew 3:16 that the Spirit of God descended from heaven like a dove and settled on Jesus after he came out of the water of his baptism.)

The question arose in my mind the other day: Will we see God Almighty when we go to heaven? I know believers will see Jesus and join the angels in worshipping God. Reading Isaiah 6 brought this up. **I'm convicted of having unclean lips, which is a reflection of an unclean heart.** The angel purified Isaiah's lips with a hot coal from the altar of the temple of God. Isaiah was then ready for special service to the Lord as His prophet. God sent him *willingly* as a messenger despite his painful awareness of sin.

I want to learn, understand, and obey all that God is speaking. I sense He's rearranging my heart and tearing out pride. My workplace ministry is also under construction. Is the season over? Am I trying to force things to grow?

I release this to you, Lord. I *trust* you during this season and ask you to *purify* my lips and heart to serve and praise you *more*!

August 16, 2014 [Answered Prayers/Attacks]

My coworker Robert and neighbor Dana were both on my heart this week. I wanted to text them but decided to wait, per the Holy Spirit. On Wednesday Robert texted me, and the next day, Dana sent a picture from Niagara Falls! It's been weeks since I have heard from her, but I pray for her all the time. Another kiss from God!

Something that I wanted to share from last Sunday—I received an email from Nancy, a possible mentor! Not only was that *so* uplifting but her email was sent at 11:40 a.m., which was about the time that I was praying for a mentor at the IBC altar! Isn't that amazing? I knew then that this lady may be the one God has chosen.

I met Nancy Friday on my lunch break and experienced heavy spiritual warfare; it was nearly unbearable the first ten minutes. Why? The bait that Satan used to distract me at work was there! Yup, Jim was seated at a booth facing us. As we followed the hostess, I thought, *Oh no! She's going to seat us at the table next to them!* Thank God she didn't.

I shared a lot in our first meeting and couldn't cut off the flow! I hope Nancy wasn't overwhelmed. The enemy attacked the rest of the day, saying I shouldn't have said this or that; "I talked too much"; "I didn't listen well"; and "I was selfish and a fool." I repented if I said anything that was too strong or passionate.

August 23, 2014 [Hugging my Hero]

My mind is full of truth and brain knowledge from the 7-hour conference. I went alone and met Shannon from Canada. We both love travel, health, Jane Austen movies, and nature. Our best friends recently married, and we're seeking new friends. I thank God for her companionship!

All attendees received Dr. Leaf's autographed book, *Switch On Your Brain*. Anxiety may be the next root that needs to be destroyed. I have mild social anxiety (crowded rooms), work anxiety, and relational anxiety.

The best part, other than meeting Shannon, was meeting Dr. Leaf! I didn't know what to say but prayed the Holy Spirit would direct me. When it was my turn, I said, "I'm going to hug you. Is that okay?" My heart was so grateful. I first heard her speak at the Joyce Meyer conference, "Mind, Mouth, Mood, and Attitude." I told her she was my science hero and she smiled. I felt such love for her and her calling. What an honor to meet her!

August 26, 2014 [Dream Come True]

I flipped through my seminar journal, and my eyes fell on notes from last September. I wrote answers to: Where would you like to live? Who would you like to meet? **There it was in my own handwriting—a dream that I had forgotten about.** The answer was "Dr. Caroline Leaf." In that moment, I realized what God had done for me! He knows the desires of our hearts. He's faithful if we will only trust Him!

Meeting Shannon was a *huge* blessing. We have so much in common: childhood teasing, distant fathers, living as nonbelievers, accepting Jesus as adults, and experiencing life transformation. We live far apart but we connected on a deep level. She had prayed for a new friend at the conference and so did I! God answered our prayers quickly because we met as soon as we got in line to enter the room. She invited me to Canada once her home is built.

God has blessed me so much lately—Nancy the mentor, Shannon the friend, and meeting Dr. Leaf! Praise the Lord! God is *amazing*!

August 29, 2014 [Sharing My Faith]

Nancy came over tonight and we had a great conversation. She said to come over next Friday. I'm so humbled. The enemy had me doubting her interest, and now I see she's committed to getting to know me. Praise God!

Another praise: I shared my faith with a male coworker!
I mentioned the Dr. Leaf conference and rewiring the brain,
which led to the topic of God. He was raised Catholic but is
open to all religions as a way of moral integrity. We talked
for forty minutes [uninterrupted with no one around us]. The
Holy Spirit gave me courage to share about Jesus, the Bible
being the Word of God, and the Spirit giving understanding. **I
tried to explain that man created religion, but it's having a
relationship with Jesus that changes and heals us.**

I walked away encouraged that we were open and vulnerable
and that we respected each other's beliefs. I *know* the Lord
planted seeds in his heart, and I asked 3 people to pray [that he
would receive Jesus as His Savior]. I was *so* excited driving
home. I felt alive! The Lord is moving at my workplace!

I've had attacks in my mind since meeting Nancy, Dr. Leaf,
and Shannon. All 3 are big answers to prayer in such a short time!

September 8, 2014 [Going to the Altar]

Saturday, I met [my potential mentee] for coffee. She's
twenty-one and pursuing a degree in Psychology. God will
need to direct me, because I'm new to being a mentor.

Sunday, I met Tierny [coworker] at IBC. After the service,
I recognized a lady from spin class and introduced myself.
Helen lives one minute away from my house in Lewisville!

God is good. I woke up early, excited about my mentor, my
mentee, and Helen. God has answered my prayers in the past
30 days. **I will continue fasting and praying at the altar at
church. Too many blessings to stop now!** Thank you, Lord!

September 10, 2014

I was up before 4:00 a.m. and started my study on Joshua.
Class tonight was great! I shared [in the small group session]
that Joshua meditated on the Word of God, and when Jen
Wilkin spoke in the sanctuary, she said the focal point of
chapter one was meditating on the Book of the Law.

I signed the repair contract for [a foundation company] to install 7 piers in the back of my house and a sixty-foot combo drain (surface and French drain).

September 14, 2014

I'm tired from getting less sleep. God has awakened me before my alarm the past several days. One day I was up at 3:30 a.m.! My mood on Friday was sour, and I blamed the cold, rainy weather. This is day 3 of cloudy skies. I think my period is due to start, or **God's testing my heart and I'm failing for lack of humility and thankfulness.**

Saturday was Kids Night Out at IBC [a single-parent event]. I really wanted to stay home to rest, but I prayed for an attitude change and went anyway. I talked with a sweet single mom whom I had met before. I asked if I could pray with her. I took her hand in my hands and prayed for direction and open doors. That experience blessed me and was definitely better than resting on the couch!

September 22, 2014 [First Marriage Conference]

Glorious! I am on my patio on my day off with a blanket over my shoulders, breezes through my trees, planes overhead, and a bird or two in the distance. I am the only human—or so it feels!

I attended a coworker's marriage conference. It was a great event and a delight to meet his brothers. Intercessory prayer for singles was at the end, and his brother the bishop stopped in front of me. **While my coworker's wife was praying for marriage for the single woman next to me, the bishop prayed about my talents and gifts developing, especially in the next 3 weeks.**

My prayer intensity has increased regarding ministry and friendships. I'm waiting to hear from my new friend Shannon since my last email; and I haven't seen Helen, my mentor, or my mentee in two weeks. I desire these friendships to grow.

God encouraged me yesterday. Synergy [class at church] was great—I went alone and sat with several nice couples. I know the Lord has removed friends to replace them with God's people.

September 29, 2014 [Holy Spirit Moving]
Oh my goodness! My brother and I had a great conversation while he was at the airport. I had his undivided attention for forty-five minutes. He started with, "What's been going on in your life?" By the grace of God and the power of the Holy Spirit, I told him. I shared about the marriage conference, God removing friends, and my Jen Wilkin Bible study.

He asked some good questions—even one about homosexuality. Having read *Loveology*, **God prepared me to answer that question, speaking the truth in love.** The Holy Spirit directed my words, and seeds were planted in his heart.

I shared about Synergy's couples and how growing up without knowing aunts, uncles, and grandparents, I desire those types of relationships now. It's amazing how God used my experiences to work in his heart [and mind]! My testimony of how God is working in my life is to be *shared*. God will water the seeds.

I took my Maxima to the Dallas dealership. I prayed for the Holy Spirit to show me what to do regarding the suggested repairs: 3 motor mounts, front struts, and rear shocks. **God answered as I went through my paperwork and took a few days to pray.** The recommended repairs were *different* from the ones the Lewisville dealership recommended in May: power steering pump, six ignition coils, and a drive belt! I have gone to the Nissan dealership in Lewisville for fourteen years, and flipping through my stack of repairs, I realized that I had been deceived—the front struts and drive belts had been replaced twice! God opened my eyes. I won't take my car to either dealership again. I picked it up without having any repairs.

Praise for the conversation with my brother! Praise for the truth about my car!

October 4, 2014

God has blessed me so much that I can barely keep track! Tom [a fatherly man at church] and I spoke after Synergy. He'd like to have lunch sometime! Of course, his wife Sue will join us, whom I adore! I prayed last week that they would adopt me into their family or have an interest in getting to know me. Answered prayer!

October 5, 2014 [Exploding with Blessings]

After Synergy, Tom invited me to sit with him and Sue for the service. I accepted gladly. ☺ He asked if we can connect on Facebook, and his friend request arrived at 3:33 p.m. Triple 3's—seems God-ordained to me!

Today's message was on singleness. Pastor Andy called Christian singles "God's Delta Force"; delta is the symbol for change (i.e., change agents). **We are essential, fruitful, and deserving of God's family.**

After service, I met my mentee for lunch. A lady from IBC's summer study came over to say how much she and the other ladies enjoyed the Joyce Meyer teachings I gave them. She shared her CD with her daughters, and the ladies plan to swap and share! Totally *God* moving; I was only the instrument.

Renee asked how I am doing and I replied that I feel like a new creature, a butterfly emerging from the cocoon. I'm exploding with joy and laughter, praising God to and from work. *God is moving strongly.*

Another amazing story: I was the only woman out of 500 to let Jen Wilkin know about an error in our homework. I believe others had noticed it, but I was the only one to speak up. She announced at the next lecture, "Charlotte was the only brave soul" to approach her and pointed in my direction.

October 10, 2014 [Birthday Battle]

Oh, how quickly things can change.

Birthdays are getting harder for me emotionally. It's the *one* day I want to feel loved, and the enemy was all over me with doubt, disappointment, and despair. Every suppressed emotion from the past year surfaced—I cried twice.

Last week I was hurt when [3 church friends didn't respond to my texts or emails]. I am too downcast to open my two birthday cards. I resumed Facebook for 3 days and my peace is gone—coincidence? I found myself obsessing over the number of birthday posts, which is bad.

My coworkers nearby didn't wish me a happy birthday, but one baked cookies and someone put balloons all over my desk. I probably should be grateful, but [another coworker] got cookies, cheesecake, two birthday signs, streamers, balloons, *and* people stopped by to wish him a happy birthday. I confess to being disappointed.

I know my self-worth is not linked to how people treat me or how many FB posts I get. I am loved by God the Father, Creator of heaven and earth. I know in my heart that my family loves me, but I often feel neglected. My primary love language is quality time, and I get little of their attention.

Today is Friday, and I should be at work. I've hardly slept the past two nights. I needed time with the Lord to desperately understand and handle my emotions. In addition to my disappointments with people, I am grieving $8,500 of foundation repair that will be done next week. It took me years to save. I wanted new carpeting or to travel to Europe. My car needs repairs and new tires—more expenses!

Lord Jesus, please help me reclaim my identity in Christ as your precious child. I am loved by many and your love is enough. Help me believe that today. I know it's true, but my feelings are pulling me off course. You have a plan and purpose for every trial and triumph. I know that I'm making a difference for your kingdom. Rescue me!

October 18, 2014 [House Battle]

My mind is overwhelmed. The foundation repair company installed 7 piers to lift the back of my house. I still have anxiety now that the job is finished because the sixty-foot combination drain was a huge ordeal. There were mistakes and confusion regarding the drainage pipes, and yet I trusted the foreman when he told me it was fixed.

I'm grateful my parents were here for both moral and financial support. This ordeal has been emotionally draining, and I have had to fight off worry, fear, and paranoia. They are a reputable company with an "A" rating from the Better Business Bureau. Now I wait six months to a year for my house to settle [and for my foundation to adjust].

I *pray* this is the *last* of my foundation issues! Nine piers in the front, 7 in the back, and a combo drain on the side; the grand total is $13,000! **Who knows but God how long I will live in this house?** Right now, life is so full that dating and marriage are the furthest thing on my mind. Honestly.

Next up is sprinkler adjustment, fence gate realigning, and sewer line plumbing repairs; then next year will be drywall repairs, repainting, and fence staining.

October 26, 2014

I'm on my patio with a blanket enjoying a still morning. Mom put a scarecrow in my backyard [as an autumn decoration]; I don't know if it will keep my doves away. They seem to gather in my oak tree in the evenings.

I've noticed many butterflies the past two weeks. Whenever I turn around or look up, one flutters by. **During my season of metamorphosis, I know the butterfly is God's reminder to me that He is at work making something beautiful.**

There are two unresolved issues with my foundation repair—I spent 3 hours drafting an email to the owner. I *pray* for a proper and fair resolution and trust that God will be my vindicator.

November 3, 2014 [Holy Spirit Nudges]

I am exhausted. This is week 3 after the foundation repair. Week one was spent emailing and texting the foundation repair salesman. Week two was spent writing and waiting on the owner's responses. He denied all my requests except one. His tone was rude and defensive. I wrote a passionate rebuttal, and his next response was kinder.

I prayed for God to deal with the owner in his conscience and for the truth to be known. If he knows I am right, he's not coming forward. **The Holy Spirit woke me up** on Friday about the gravel, and again on Sunday about the concrete patches. The Spirit had nudged me to take a picture of the French drain in progress, but I didn't.

Stephen Meyer, PhD in Philosophy of Science from Cambridge University, spoke at all 3 IBC services. He also hosted a lecture about the fossil explosion. Fossils didn't evolve, but suddenly appeared. He discussed the genetic code and how improbable it is for nonlethal mutations to occur early in the animal development, and yet be significant enough to be passed along to create a new genetic code.

A neat thing happened when Dr. Meyer searched for a water bottle on the podium. He looked up asking, "Does anyone have a bottle of water that I may have?" Immediately, I reached into my bag. **I usually pack two bottles when I go somewhere; but this time, the Holy Spirit nudged me to take 3!** I glanced around to see if someone else was on their way to the front. I didn't see anyone so I stood up, walked twenty feet to the stage, and handed him the bottle. All I remember was looking at his hand and hearing him say, "Thank you." Too cool! There were over 300 people present. I was so tired that I almost didn't go. God used me again to bless someone. Love it! ☺

November 22, 2014 [Lord Speaks Life]

The good news is that I see a light at the end of my tunnel of darkness and oppression. Since the drain installation and email exchanges with the owner, I have lacked peace and sound sleep. He remains unchanged, claiming that all was done correctly and that I am "paranoid" and "obsessed."

Praise the Lord for showing me the way out! When I came home from the gym two weeks ago God said to me, "What's the biggest source of stress the past two years?" I answered, "My house." He replied, "Then why don't you sell it?" Instantly, I felt peace. Suddenly, and for the *first* time, I wanted to sell my house.

I found a real estate agent. He's confident my house will sell after the repairs are done. I like the idea of a townhouse with no yard maintenance. I should earn enough from my house sale for both a down payment and a new car. What a blessing! Now I'm praying for an affordable sewer line repair and resolution to the drain issue. Oh, the freedom of getting out of here!

Lord, show me the way and the place you have for me! Is it Grapevine, Lewisville, Coppell, Flower Mound, or other?

Things at work are good. Our client contract will be renewed through December 2015.

November 24, 2014 [People Pain]

I'm supposed to be at work today but have not been sleeping well for days. I'm overwhelmed and feel out of control. I submitted my last response [regarding the drain issue].

Oh, Lord, I pray you are using this for your glory somehow. Help me endure, and bring proper resolution!

I called two Christian counselors today and left messages. I'm finally ready to seek outside help. I don't question God's love or His plan for my life. **My struggle is ordained by the Lord; He's refining me like gold.** It just feels so heavy at times—the disappointments with friends, family, and fellow Christians. I feel like an orphan lately —living alone, walking the narrow path, learning to love people and manage my own pain with little encouragement.

You know I adore Sue and Tom; however, I'm not as close to them as I want to be. They are very active in the church and have many friends. I secretly wish they would adopt me, but there are *no* signs of this happening. They chat with me on Sundays, but where do I fit into their lives? Am I just another single lady they have befriended at church? **For some crazy reason, I thought they may like me enough to introduce me to their son.** My heart aches over this; I cannot make anyone love me. I continue waiting on God and carrying my cross forward.

Should I continue Synergy? There are many nice couples, but none show an interest in getting to know me personally. Last Sunday, Kate spoke at Synergy and said to let her know if anyone had information on neuroscience regarding thoughts and words. I got excited to share about Dr. Leaf, and I wrote my name, email, and cell number on a piece of paper. I handed it to her after class, expecting her to contact me or speak with me the following Sunday. All I received was a LinkedIn request. I lay this at the feet of Jesus. I really wanted to share my story and excitement of Dr. Leaf's research.

Here's everything I'm laying down at the feet of Jesus:

- Sue and Tom
- Kate and Dr. Leaf
- Parents, brother, and family
- French drain issue
- Townhouse and moving
- Sewer line leak
- Desire for godly friends
- Desire for spiritual family
- My bank account
- My life, my heart, my soul
- Yearning to be loved, accepted, and understood

November 27, 2014 [Blown Away]

I'm on the plane to San Antonio for Thanksgiving.

The past few days have been odd and deeply emotional. Tuesday was hard, since I returned to the office without seeing a counselor. I was on the verge of tears and anger, almost at the edge of my sanity. I know that my circumstances are ordered by the Lord, to break me down to rebuild me for *His* glory. That's hard to explain to people; even Christians don't necessarily understand. Perhaps the counselor will. I meet with her on December 3 at 3:00 p.m.

My latest God story: I was really struggling on Tuesday. I replied to Tom's Facebook message, and at the *same* time, he sent me a text. He wanted to talk, so we met the next day for lunch. After our plates were cleared, he told me what he wanted to share. Tom didn't want to seem presumptuous, but felt he knew me well enough to see my heart. He knows the heart of his son as well and feels we should be introduced, somehow, someday, someway! Obviously, we don't know the Lord's will, but I was *so* encouraged that Tom shared a desire that the Lord put on *my* heart a few months ago! How amazing is that?!? He said if I visit New York, his son and I could meet casually for a meal without him knowing the background. [Tom didn't know that Jasmine and I had discussed going to NYC just 3 days earlier!]

As we walked to our cars, Tom stopped and said, "I mean this in the most authentic, godly, fatherly way possible… I really do love you." *OMG!* I prayed that God would give Tom and Sue a love for me. **There it was, unsolicited, a prayer answered!** Even if his son does not love me, Tom does. He's like a wonderful father to me—kind, joyous, prayerful, and a good listener. I said that I loved him too and we hugged in the parking lot, like a scene from a movie. *How* incredible is that? This *has* to be God's doing, His will in His timing. Thank you, Jesus! I am so *humbled* and *amazed* that what started as a crazy thought, a miracle of sorts, may actually become reality. Part of my life story, God's perfect plan.

Glory to God, I think I may explode! Yet all of this is uncertain, to be revealed in His time.

December 16, 2014

My realtor is showing my house to a cash buyer now. I received a letter last week from a local realtor regarding her cash buyer. Sounds too good to be true! The timing is incredible, if it be God's will. **I prayed for the right buyer to come at the right time.**

After Synergy, Jasmine, Sue, Tom, and I sat together for the service. Pastor Barry taught that when God "interrupts" our lives with His plan, we have a choice to obey or go our own way. Afterwards, Sue and Tom drove us to a Christmas concert at the oldest Christian church in Fort Worth. Tom and I walked back to his car to get my purse. We had a great conversation, laughing as we walked through the rain sharing an umbrella. It was a precious time. God is *so* good.

December 17, 2014

3:30 a.m.
The showing went well. My realtor and I agreed on a listing price. Now I wait and pray for God's will to be done.

5:45 p.m.
Still waiting on the buyer's response; waiting is *hard*! God knows the outcome, so this is a good exercise in trusting Him.

December 18, 2014

Their offer is reasonable but my realtor thinks we can do better. I must reflect on my counter offer. It's hard to not get emotional/anxious/nervous with each step.

Last Thursday, I had received this cash buyer's letter. The next day, I got a voice mail from Joyce Meyer Ministries thanking me for my partnership and saying they were praying for me! The timing is incredible. **Here I sit, 7 days later, with a potential buyer for my home!**

Since my lunch with Tom, I'm seeing and hearing "New York" almost daily. The coat I wore that day was "Jones New York." Dr. Tony Evans began his radio message with a New York City reference. A mailed perfume sample was "DKNY New York." My new tote bag says "Coach New York," and I hadn't noticed for 3 weeks!

Two days ago, I drove to work in a daze. I noticed the license plate in front of me—New York! A few minutes later, I flipped on Classical 101.1 FM and they were playing the Bridal Chorus (da-duh-duh-da). I listened for 3 minutes before I connected "New York" and "wedding." Later that day, my heart filled with love for a man I have never met—Tom's son. The thought of living in New York is overwhelming, and it's too cold, wet, and gray for my preference. But if that's where I belong, the Lord will give me grace to go there.

January 1, 2015 [Breaking News]

Where do I start? He has a girlfriend. I found out by seeing a photo on Facebook! Tom said he was shocked and had *no* idea. I hope our friendship won't be affected. I still believe God brought Tom and me together for a reason. God gave me 3 desires that were confirmed when we met in November: (1) Sue and Tom's love; (2) meet their son; and (3) visit New York. If I believe God's at work, then I must believe this girlfriend is not his future wife.

I had 3 plumbers come out—one quoted the sewer line repair at $1,450 *per* leak and there are two!!! He's booked 30 days out, and I can't sell the house until it's fixed.

More drama: I'm dissatisfied with my realtor [for a variety of reasons]. I'm also leaning toward renting an apartment in Grapevine.

January 10, 2015 [Path Revealed!]

The cash buyer walked away.

The plumber is coming the week of the 19th. I pray the second leak is small enough to ignore. Please, Lord! He's going to jack hammer the slab under the guest toilet and tear up my floor. The drywall estimate is $950. If I take off work, I lose $800. **I can't focus on what I'm losing. I must focus on what I'm gaining at the end of this hailstorm—freedom to serve God.** It won't be easy or comfortable—moving, readjusting, and downsizing—but in the end, it will be worth it. This is a trial of mass proportions, so I need more time with God. I need Him to hold me up, to calm my anxious heart, and to lead me through the water. Praise Him in the storm!

Twelve years in this house—I have too much stuff. I am volunteering to die to self every day and it hurts. I want all the answers now: Who's going to buy my furniture? How much do I give away? Am I spending my time wisely? I feel no desire for social activities.

Work is steady, redoing client requests 3 times for all of 3rd quarter. It's out of my control. Lord, *help* me trust you and stay *calm*!

The Lord led me to an apartment in Grapevine! I found it on the internet. They had 3 apartments on the 3rd floor coming available in mid-March, but only *one* had the nature view. The girl showed me two models; I liked one immediately. It must have been the Holy Spirit, because as soon as she opened the door, before I saw anything, I felt an instant "yes!" It was strong. I knew this was where God wants me—a one bedroom apartment in Grapevine! I had prayed in December and felt that Grapevine was where I needed to be, but no townhomes were available. That was good, since the Lord is leading me to rent and not own.

I drove back the next day. I realized that I can impact more people for the kingdom by living in an apartment—more common areas. While at the leasing office, I met a girl who had broken up with her boyfriend of 7 years, and they

were still living together. God's preparing my heart. I took
pictures inside the model apartment and then walked to
the back of Building 19. I couldn't see my future balcony,
but it faced trees.☺ Praise God! Standing there, my heart
rejoiced. I'm so *grateful* and *thankful* for the Holy Spirit's
leading!

When I got home, I noticed the first photo I took had a
cross beaming out of the lamp! I zoomed in. It was not part of
the lampshade. It was created by *light* from the bulb filtered
through the fabric! I then realized that I had prayed Psalm
25:4-5 all weekend: "Show me the path where I should walk,
O Lord, point out the right road for me to follow. Lead me by
your truth and teach me, for you are the God who saves me."
He answered that prayer—twice!

One more thing—I wrote Tom an email last week. The day
he had reached out to me in November, he had a very strong
and clear desire for me to meet his son. I shared that the Lord
had given me the *same* desire a month earlier. We agreed there
was nothing to do but pray for his son to seek the Lord and
for God's will to be done. A renewed peace evolved. God's
working, and it's going to take time to unfold.

January 11, 2015 [Say What?]

Great day! I woke up early and spent time with the Lord. I
felt extra good on my way to church. Jasmine didn't make

it, so I had Sue and Tom all to myself.☺ I told them about my apartment. A married lady introduced herself as I sat down. She asked if I was related to Sue and Tom, if I was their daughter-in-law!?! I responded, "Friend." **I wondered if that was the Holy Spirit speaking through her.** After class I asked Tom, "She knows your son's not married, right?" He replied, "Yes, she knows. I don't know why she asked that."

January 16, 2015 [3ʳᵈ Distraction]

It's 12:55 p.m. and I can't sleep. Carlos has hurt me. He's the 33-year-old Columbian who's been flirting with me at work. [I am embarrassed to admit that] it's another test! First was Pete, second was Jim, and guy number 3 is Carlos. Not sure what's in his heart, but I got sucked in for a few weeks.

Oh, Lord, help me to forgive and let go. Help me to be kind whenever I see him. Help me to be his sister in Christ.

February 1, 2015

Good Sunday morning! Today is IBC's celebration for paying off $9 million of mortgage debt! Now we can fund more ministries and expand our medical clinic. I'm here now, alone and very early. Jasmine thought she was coming but went into work.

Here's the latest:

- Carlos is married!!! A coworker told me *and* he hits on her in the breakroom too! I'm shocked. He's real smooth. He fooled me. He needs Jesus. I will continue praying for him.

- I hired a new realtor, Terri, who sings in the IBC choir. She thinks I can get $10,000 more, since the market's going up. **God's Hand is in all of this!** He knows *who* my buyer is and *when* they are coming.

- Plumber fixed sewer lines for $2,800 and both bathrooms need new flooring.

- My parents are coming the week before my move. It will be during spring break, and my nieces will be off school— Praise! I didn't plan it that way, nor did I consider it a possibility. The Lord gave me the move-in date!

February 15, 2015

The drywall cracks are repaired and the new floors look great. The bill was $4,700. Tomorrow Francisco repairs the frieze boards. I pray the rain will hold off so it doesn't affect the repair.

My neighbors sold their house on the *first* day for more than their asking price! **I continue to pray for the right buyer to come at the right time and offer the right price.** It's all in the Lord's hands!

February 19, 2015 [Answered Prayer]

Francisco worked outside when it was below freezing. I'm in awe! He did *more* than quoted and for such a low price. He was truly the best man for the job! Praise the Lord! A missionary handyman painted the frieze boards and touched up my front door. I'm thankful for him and Francisco!

Yesterday Terri listed my house for sale at 9:06 a.m. The first showing request came at 9:30 a.m.; and by 11:00 a.m., I had 3 showings. Then it was 7, ten, thirteen, *fourteen*, all for that day! ☺ Today there are six showings.

February 21, 2015 [Right Buyer/Answered Prayers]

Today is Saturday, the final day of showings. Terri presented me with 7 offers—five are above list price! She talked through each one. One buyer had the strongest overall offer and was going above and beyond to make things easier for me. The only concern was her lender; Terri had had bad experiences with them in the past. So I picked this buyer hoping she would change lenders.

When we hung up, I walked into my kitchen. Dong had given me a red envelope that morning for Chinese New Year.

It was lying face down on the counter. I turned it over and on the front of the bank envelope it said, "[Buyer's lender]." Right then I realized that I had prayed for the Lord's direction as to which buyer to pick; **I had made my selection, and within seconds the Lord confirmed it!**

Then I sensed the Lord may also be saying to use *this* lender and not another. When I discovered the buyer works there and gets an added incentive, I felt okay using them. Terri called to speak with a loan officer, but it was after 5:00 p.m. [and she didn't expect anyone to answer]. While she called, I prayed the Lord would direct her thoughts so she would get a clear indication if we should accept this lender or wait for another. The officer told Terri everything she wanted to hear: he's local and handles the entire loan processing, and he provided his direct contact info. She felt good, and I was elated! Answered prayer! Thank you, Jesus!

I am in *awe* how the Lord has fine-tuned the details to unfold in my favor! The offered price being $10,000 *above* list, securing the earlier closing date, finding discounted moving boxes, receiving a friend's referral for a moving company, learning that my parents are coming to help, selling four of my tables to a neighbor, Terri buying my sofa bed—not to mention Francisco's amazing repair and the missionary handyman who caulked and painted the day before we listed. I'm blown away! Everything is falling into place. Praise the Lord!

March 4, 2015

We are waiting on the appraisal. I'm praying that I get the full offer price.

My parents arrive Saturday, and closing is set for the 18th. Much to do between now and then! I'm trusting God to control the details and guide my steps.

My IBC small group started; there are twelve of us. I really need a spiritual family.

Friday night was a struggle. More snow! I was stuck inside again. I had plenty to do—pack, clean, purge—but didn't feel up to it. Instead, I poured my heart out to God and shed tears for the desires of my heart that are yet to be met.

Big praise—the foundation passed inspection!!! Thank you, Lord!

March 15, 2015 [My Sanctuary]

I am writing from my new apartment in Grapevine! I'm sitting up in bed on a cool morning, listening to a bird singing outside my window! What a *huge* praise to be in *this* particular apartment! I have a view of trees through 3 of the four windows!

Last night, we returned from dinner to discover the sun setting outside my balcony! The sky was a bright pink and the horizon flat and clear. Pinkish light streamed in through the windows, illuminating my wall. It was like a kiss from God: "Welcome home, my Love."

March 16, 2015

My *view* is breathtaking! I gave up six mature trees and a patio [at my house] for woods and a covered balcony. Wow! This is more peaceful and beautiful than I had imagined! Bless the Lord for leading me here. I am so happy!

March 24, 2015

Mom and Dad returned to San Antonio on Sunday. I'm writing from my balcony. Quiet and still. The hum of AC units and planes are in the distance. Two flocks of birds flew by in V-formation. The sky is cloudy with pink, white, and patches of blue. My hawk friend is circling the golf course. This is the 3rd day in a row spotting him. I'm in awe. **I prayed for one or two trees and the Lord gave me a forest!** There's even an Eifel Tower on the horizon (radio tower).

Every day I get more settled. My soul feels free. This is my Neverland. Praise the Lord! There are no words to describe this place. It's surreal, like the Garden of Eden. A large white bird flew by—a crane? Wow! I need to get binoculars.

April 10, 2015 [Sharing My Story]

Last weekend, I met Sue and Tom for Good Friday service. They came over and we talked on my balcony for nearly two hours. Tom asked how I came to Christ and I shared my story. I had a wonderful time and probably talked too much.

April 12, 2015

I celebrated Easter at the 9:30 service with Helen from spin class. Worship was great! I thought the roof was going to blow off when we sang "Great I Am." **There was incredible energy and presence of the Lord—all of His children praising Him in a packed house. Wow!**

I went to [a couple's home] for Easter dinner. I had a wonderful time and was reminded how beautiful extended family dinners can be. Sadly, I never knew them. My brother and I sat at the "kids table," even when there weren't other kids to play with.

Small group was awkward, but the whole morning felt that way. Afterwards, Tom told me that he wanted to talk—things are going well for [his son and girlfriend]. Both are very happy and in love. They are coming to Texas the 3rd weekend in May. *Lord, have mercy!* My heart nearly split in Robbie and Julie's house. Tom said he was very sorry, and he still loves me. Tears were in his eyes and mine.

Honestly, I'm hurting and angry. Why would the Lord speak to Tom and me about meeting his son in the same month that he met his girlfriend? There's no engagement yet, but it's heading that way. Lord, I need you. *Help!*

April 18, 2015 [Divine Refund]

Thank you, Lord, for redeeming the $20,000 spent on major house repairs! [*]

[*By not selling to the cash buyer in December, and with the housing market increasing through February, and with my house selling for $9,000 above my asking price, the Lord returned *all* of the money I had spent on foundation repairs, sewer line leaks, dry-wall repairs, etc. It blew me away! Money that I thought was wasted and gone forever was returned!]

April 21, 2015 [Prayer and Fasting]

I'm fasting from sweets for forty days or until the Lord directs otherwise. I pray for God's will to be done in Tom's son's life. I don't believe that God would speak to Tom and me separately about the same desires and not fulfill them.

Today I meet Stacey from the Stephens Ministry. I pray that I won't cry. I pray the Holy Spirit directs my words, because my emotions are up and down and all over lately. Truth is constant. Our emotions are not.

Tom read my testimony and said I'm "a great writer." He has written at least one book that I know of, so that means a lot for him to say that. I shared that I have kept journals since elementary school and **desire to write a book** highlighting the *amazing* things the Lord has done in me, for me, and through me.

April 30, 2015 [Alumni Visit]

I turn thirty-nine this year, but I feel younger inside. It's like the closer I grow to God, the more childlike I become. This may be a good sign.

Last weekend I went to Ann Arbor, Michigan, to reunite with Lisa and Steff. We met at Angelo's for breakfast and then drove to North Campus to tour the Dow Building. Lecture room 1013 looked the same! It felt surreal. Seventeen years ago, we graduated from the University of Michigan; **I was a completely different person.** I studied my guts out and somehow graduated cum laude! I definitely felt like I didn't belong there. Chemical Engineering was not my true calling.

May 16, 2015

Small group has two more meetings, and Synergy has paused for summer. I welcome the break but will miss my small group. Tomorrow I host them at 6:00 p.m. **We are praying for a beautiful sunset; the forecast is severe weather.** The past 3 days have been partly cloudy and humid.

Tom's son and girlfriend are here, so I will skip church; it's best for everyone if I don't see or meet them. I was fasting, but now I'm semi-fasting as I pray for God's will.

Speak, Lord, to his heart *clearly* so he will understand your divine will. Please hear my prayer! Give me grace to accept whatever happens next.

May 20, 2015

Our work project ends December 2015. Part of me hopes to get laid off. Why? To write my book, my life story with focus on God's blessings, trials, and triumphs.

For the first time in my life, I am actually at peace with dying. There have been times when I've wanted God to bring me home to heaven. I'm not close with family, I feel distant from friends, I'm unmarried, and I have no children, so my attachments to this world are few.

I have stopped praying for Tom's son. I've let him go and hope to soon forget. [*]

[*I was sad because what I strongly believed was God's plan, confirmed by Tom, disintegrated before my eyes. I wanted Tom and Sue as my in-laws, and since I loved them so much, it seemed natural for me to love their son as well.]

Members of my small group came over on Sunday and left by 8:00 p.m. One couple wanted to stay for the sunset [which was the reason for meeting at night] but felt awkward since everyone else had left. The Lord delivered a beautiful sunset with clear skies and perfect temps [and yet I watched it alone]. I was disappointed, deeply. I didn't sleep well, feeling let down by the group. Could they not linger twenty minutes to watch with me?

May 22, 2015 [Prompted to Pray]

As I lay awake on Sunday night, Matthew 26:40 kept going through my mind: Can you not stay awake even one hour to pray?

Since April, I've begun noticing the numbers 3 and 33—I flew to Michigan out of gate C33, seat C31, baggage claim 3. I gassed up my car for exactly $33.00 [it stopped on its own when the tank was full]. Lisa's sister had just canned 33 jars of jam. Beltline Road is exit 33 [the road to Irving Bible Church]. Yesterday, I glanced at the clock at 5:33 a.m., 6:33 a.m. and 7:33 a.m.!

Jasmine and I prayed for the Lord to reveal His message to me. She shared about Anne Graham Lotz's Mayday! Prayer Initiative. Anne is calling all followers of Jesus to pray for America and for the church to unite in one accord for the harvesting of souls for His kingdom. Recently, Anne taught a prophecy seminar; and when she finished, she *knew* God spoke through her. **Judgment is coming on America and our world. It's going to be horrible.** Author Joel Rosenberg delivered a message from Ezekiel *33*—the responsibility we bear to respond to the truth. Christians must be watchmen, delivering the warning to the lost.

I visited Anne's website, hoping this was the message from the Lord to me. All those 33s increasing in frequency. The first comment below her blog referenced Matthew 26:40, the verse that had stayed in my mind! I watched the teachings for Days 7, Six, and Five at home. Today is Day Eight.

The excessive rain and gray skies have left me feeling blue. My small group disappointment, news of the girlfriend, and other things are challenging my faith. I'm seeking God's direction for how to spend my time and who to spend it with. Do I join a Bible study? Take a seminary class? Try ballet? Is it time to replace Maximus? I've spent $900 on repairs and new tires. **I'm letting go of what lies behind and pressing on to the good things ahead.**

I met with Stacey last month at IBC and was honest about my ache for godly friends and a spiritual family. She said

that I didn't need a Stephen minister but thought I would
make a good one! [Stephen Ministry is a one-to-one lay
caring ministry where a caregiver meets with a hurting person
going through a tough season in life.] Stacey confirmed my
connection with God is rare. She's a wise lady who has been
involved in ministry a long time; I trust she's correct. I still
feel alone.

June 14, 2015 [His Return]
My soul is at rest, as I sit on the balcony listening to birds
while conversing with God. I'm waiting on Him to direct me
regarding the 33s—a breakroom microwave displayed 0:33
minutes; a previous customer's gasoline sale was $22.33; my
statement had a balance with 33 cents; I later realized one of
my work passwords ends in "33." That blew me away!

   According to "Bible Study.org," the number 33 reflects
both God's promises and God's judgment! **Jesus promised
He is coming again [to judge the world].** I typed a list of
daily 33 occurrences and revelations since May. There were
so many that I became tired and stopped after several weeks.
I keep seeing them, and maybe I always will. The May 18
earthquake at our office was magnitude *3.3*! Dallas had record
rainfall, the most in *33* years! God is speaking.

   Saturday, I woke up to pounding rain, lightning, and
thunder. [I lay in bed asking God, *What are you saying with
all this rain?*] Then my clock radio clicked on. A song had just
started and the first line was, "… Jesus is coming soon."

   Bible Study Fellowship is having their first Revelation
study this September! The timing is *no* coincidence: growing
social and racial unrest, storms and draught, political scandals
and fraud. Anne said when things seem out of control, they are
falling into place per God's Word.

   I desire to spend time in prayer and studying Revelation,
Joel, John, and Ezekiel (watchman for Israel). John the
Baptist lived in the wilderness and prepared the way for Jesus.

I wonder if a similar role is planned for me by God; I long to be with Him and listen to His voice.

8:00 p.m.
I don't know if I should continue small group in the fall. It's fun, but it's not meeting my need for authentic godly family. My heart aches over this; back to being an orphan. The sun is setting, the sky is beautiful, and my heart is heavy. Oh, help me, Lord!

June 20, 2015 [Code Red]
I signed up for ballet lessons for 7 weeks. The voice mail from the dance studio was 0.*33* minutes long and message *3* of *3*! I bought ballet shoes the next day. After trying on 7 pairs, the ones that fit best were $*33*.00 plus tax!!!

Texas Department of Transportation closed Grapevine Mills Parkway due to creek flooding. All 3 southbound lanes were underwater, and it took two hours to get home. The next day the northbound lanes were closed due to rising lake levels. **God moved me here to give me more of Himself and perhaps to prepare me for more challenging times ahead.** My anxiety escalated with possible apartment evacuations and Code Red alerts. *End-times!* I may be ready to go to heaven, but not for the trials and calamity leading up to it. I stopped reading in Revelation.

June 22, 2015 [Message for Me]
That's it! Mr. Anxiety has to go! I spoke with no faith yesterday; forgive me, Lord. I fed my fears by thinking and speaking about them.

I long for genuine friendships, and yet I'm trying to hold people and things loosely. What they say doesn't match what they do, even Christians.

Oh, I saw the West Bow Press advertisement *again*! It appeared at the top of the online stopwatch that I use daily at work. Previously I have seen their blue ad on other websites. This one said, **"Be bold and publish your Christian book."** Wow!

June 25, 2015 [Ballet Bust]

The sun is shining and my mood has lifted.

Ballet was a bust last night. The instructor went too fast. The class was 75 percent intermediate and 25 percent beginners ("newbies"). She catered to the intermediates and moved to the next pose before I could master the basics! I voiced my concern several times. I got frustrated and wanted to leave. The teacher called me out 3 times to correct me in front of the class. She didn't call out other names (i.e., "Charlotte and everybody"). Praise God that I arrived late and didn't pay in advance!

July 12, 2015 [New Car]

All is quiet and serene on my veranda. (Dad said it's not a balcony.) I'm reflecting on God's goodness and glory. My parents came for the holiday and I surprised them with Grapevine fireworks from my apartment.

I bought a 2015 Toyota Camry last week! [The recommended tire pressure is *33* psi!]

Last night was Dr. Leaf's presentation at Gateway Church. Thinking changes our mind; choosing builds networks; repetition establishes permanent connections and memories.

July 28, 2015

I have seen a *lot* of 33s since Friday.

I want my husband to be revealed. Lord, please send him soon! You told me *clearly* that night, "You don't have much longer to wait." That was over ten years ago!

I've grown and learned much since then. I am closer to God tenfold. He has used me in my workplace, in my family, and among friends and strangers to show His love. I've suffered in my mind and flesh to obey Him: experiencing sleepless nights, facing fear, meditating on His Word, forgiving others, and uprooting self-pity and fear of rejection. **In return, He gave me eyes to see the world differently and ears to hear His voice more clearly.** I've trusted Him to the edge of my sanity, crying out in my brokenness when I had no one to help me.

My life has been an awesome journey! I *know* the spouse He has chosen will allow us to grow closer to Jesus together.

August 7, 2015

Yesterday was special. [A church friend came over to share a heavy burden. I helped by listening, praying, and offering insight. God used me, and we both were blessed!]

August 19, 2015

I drove to Austin in 3 hours on Friday. I met my brother and youngest niece for lunch, and then we transferred the Maxima title and registration. [My brother bought my old car. I saw numerous 33s that day. One sighting blew me away: we had stopped at a traffic light, and I noticed a homeless man sleeping upright on a street corner. I said a silent prayer for him, and then noticed a *huge* "33" on the front of his shirt!]

Next month my Revelation study begins, and IBC small group and Synergy restart. I want to weigh my remaining time and volunteer more. Sue said a letter will arrive from the Stephen Ministry about serving as a caregiver. She and my mentor Nancy recommended me—what an honor!

August 21, 2015

Stacey emailed about the Stephen Ministry. She explained that I would minister to a woman in crisis: loss of a loved one, infertility, divorce, addiction, etc. There is an application and interview process.

Unless the Lord directs otherwise, I will remain at IBC and small group. Not sure about Synergy, but I may attend in September and see how I'm led.

I've sat on the veranda the past two nights talking to God. I reminded myself that He's in control, I trust Him, and He has a plan and a purpose for my life. **Things are barren now because He wants me to draw near.** God's preparing my next career, shaping my spouse, healing my soul, and more. This is my season to sow—sowing encouragement, grace, and mercy; sowing discipline, faith, and trust. This is the season to put my stones back on the altar: marriage, [ministry], church family, and friendships. Let them go at the feet of Jesus.

The Romans 12:12 scripture card that fell out of my book a few months ago is relevant: "Be glad for all God is planning for you. Be patient in trouble and *always* be prayerful" (NLT). I keep it posted at work.

Here's something that came to me (sounds like Joyce Meyer): **Breakdown or breakthrough—the choice is yours.** It is often a defining moment when we *feel* like giving up and things seem to be getting harder; but if we *decide* to hold on, we *will* break through! I've been there with my house and past jobs. Now I'm experiencing it with church and relationships.

The Kids Night Out ministry is fading. I want to find my passion that uses my gifts and talents. [I want to find my ministry.]

August 23, 2015

I'm writing from the peaceful bliss of my veranda. The tree to my left has grown several feet this summer. Grapevine lake levels have receded and the parks are reopening. School resumes tomorrow for most districts. I'm so thankful I no longer teach.

My neighbor cancelled our plans tonight, so I stayed home and roasted a rutabaga for the first time. It turned out amazing!

I want to return to my Candida diet: less sugars and starches; more vegetables, fish, and chicken.

September will be busy once BSF Bible study, small group, and Synergy kick off. I'm still praying about the Stephen Ministry.

I started watching the BBC series *Pride and Prejudice*. I'm in love with it and Mr. Darcy! Real men of dignity and honor exist today, but they are rare! **I resolve to wait for my Mr. Darcy**—a man of noble character who enjoys travel, art, music, and nature; a humble man with a kind heart and good manners.

Lord, I trust I will recognize him! Keep my eyes from looking to others for companionship.

September 4, 2015 [Growing Boldness]

God has given me peace regarding marriage, church family, ministry, and career.

I plan to leave CGC when our project ends and write my book. I pray it will take six months from start to finish, since the Holy Spirit will give me words.

There's a boldness growing inside of me—increased faith and confidence in God and less fear of man. If God is calling me to be a mouthpiece for Him, then I must draw near. What will 2016 hold? If now is my season to sow, then maybe 2016 is my season to reap.

My trip to Austin was fruitful. Seeds were planted in my family, and God is softening my heart. I'm reminded how selfish I still am at my core.

September 19, 2015

I decided to stop Synergy in exchange for quiet mornings with God.

Clay and I met for sushi over Labor Day weekend. He came to say goodbye, as he is moving to Denver. He said he'd stay in touch.

A week ago, **I thought I may step away from small group to visit other churches, smaller churches.** I want to be a part of a church family.

October 4, 2015

I'm on the balcony with a blanket and sweater. It's about 8:45 a.m. I *love* being out here every Sunday before church! Thank you, God, for this apartment and nature view. It is rest for my soul!

This year has been an emotional rollercoaster of ups and downs, waiting on God for direction, friends, and family. He's working in my heart, and I feel more compassion for my family.

I'm continuing with small group. Today is our 3ʳᵈ meeting and we are attending a 3-hour class on prayer. God is using them to show me things about myself. **I need to grow in grace and love for others without setting expectations.**

October 10, 2015

I turned thirty-nine [this month]. I felt loved! My coworkers decorated my desk, one baked cookies, and another made gluten-free cupcakes. Friends posted birthday wishes on Facebook, Renee shipped me a package, and several friends sent cards.

Today, four church friends took me to the Dallas Arboretum's pumpkin display. We had a beautiful picnic in the shade with pretty plates and napkins. It was very special. God bless them for their thoughtfulness!

October 16, 2015

Today is Friday. My brother, nieces, and parents arrive tonight [for a two-night visit].

Work is busy with our final month of testing.

Life is sweet, despite my daily challenges. I am 3 days behind with BSF homework. Our topic is suffering and persevering in Christ (Revelation 2). **My struggles are mental and with my flesh.** Carrying my cross forward and letting go of what I want: travel to Europe, ballet lessons, deeper godly friendships, husband, church family, etc.

Still praying about the Stephen Ministry; I don't know where the Lord will lead me and whether I will stay at IBC. I volunteered Saturday at my last Kids Night Out, after five and a half years. The Lord is moving me elsewhere, just like with Synergy. Both have gone dead in my heart.

November 11, 2015

My airline ticket is purchased for a Thanksgiving trip to San Antonio.

Our client project is wrapping up. As I've prayed the past few weeks, my spirit grows increasingly restless about staying here. **I feel strongly that my time here is ending and my desire to write is growing.** Being alone for days will be a challenge, but I can get out a little each day.

My Stephen Ministry interview was last Wednesday. The caregiver role is more of a listening "presence" and *not* a counselor offering advice. I'm unsure that I can do that.

November 20, 2015

I'm in Fort Worth at Buon Giorno Coffee by myself munching gluten-free pumpkin bread with a decaf cappuccino. The ambiance is fabulous! I can see myself returning here next year while I'm writing my story.

3:33 p.m.

I'm on a park bench in the Botanical Gardens. The moon is to my right and a fountain on my left. Few people are here. I love it, alone with God. I was supposed to spend the day with Jasmine. I waited an hour and then drove to Ft. Worth alone.

I release her, dear Lord. I'm sorry that I couldn't spend the day with her. I forgive her and will pray for her. In my heart, our friendship is over. Thank you, Lord, for meeting me here. You will bring good out of this. *I ♥ you!*

November 23, 2015 [Holy Spirit Moves]
Sunday was our last small group until January. I'm praying whether I should continue with IBC. I was in this spot 3 months ago. Renee suggests visiting other churches, which I should. **Maybe a smaller church in Grapevine?**
Last week:
- Stacey from IBC called to say that she and her male coleader both felt a "no" regarding my starting the Stephen Ministry in January. Praise God for answered prayer, because I felt that too! Quite strongly.

- I was reading Revelation 4 and realized the colors around God's throne are red, green, and white (ruby, emerald, and jasper)—Christmas colors!!! God picked those colors before the Bible was recorded! I shared this observation with my BSF leader. After we hung up, I stretched my arms overhead and looked up at the celling. *Red and green* wires were sticking out of the light fixture above my desk! That's God. ☺

God is so faithful! Doors have closed in my heart. He made it clear that I was *not* to continue: Synergy, Kids Night Out, Stephen Ministry, and friendship with Jasmine. He's pruning again. Pruning is painful. ☹

December 1, 2015 [Prayer for Guidance]
Here we are, in the final month of 2015! Just 30 days until I'm released from my job, and then I will begin writing and reading through old journals. I will continue BSF but sense that my time at IBC is over.
I visited Gateway Church and didn't feel the vibe—great church, nice people, but not where I need to be. This weekend I'm meeting Warren at 121 Community Church. The following Sunday I'll visit Dr. Tony Evans' church in Dallas.
I'm praying Psalm 25:4-5 again: "Show me the path I should walk, O LORD, point out the right road for me to follow.

Lead me by your truth and teach me, for you are the God who saves me. All day long, I put my hope in you" (NLT).

December 16, 2015 [Holy Spirit Leads]

After more prayer, I sense I am to step away from small group and IBC. **I believe the constant nag inside of me is the Holy Spirit leading me elsewhere.** Perhaps to a place I'll find consistent fellowship and godly friends, people who love Jesus and who will love me. [*]

[*While mature committed Christians exist in multitude at IBC, the Lord was not allowing me to connect with them because He was preparing me to move in a new direction. The same was true at Fellowship Church after eight years. I am blessed and grateful for my growth at both churches. They are part of my spiritual journey, and part of God's will for my life].

I visited Oak Cliff Bible Fellowship Church and enjoyed the service. Dr. Tony began with announcements, corporate prayer for those carrying burdens, and then his message, "Waiting on God" (where I am). He ended with an altar call for anyone weary from waiting. A coworker and I went down for prayer. After the service, we went to the visitor reception area and shook hands with Dr. Tony! I was unprepared; my mind went blank. I stood there staring at him, trying to find words to say how much I benefit from his radio broadcasts. Wow!

Oh, the CGC holiday party was at *3333* Turtle Creek Blvd.!

December 21, 2015

Lunch with Tom was only twenty minutes. I didn't have time to tell him about God leading me away from IBC. His son and girlfriend are flying in for Christmas, and their wedding is next month in the Grand Caymans.

Yesterday I visited Abundant Life Church in Grapevine. It's an Assembly of God church with one service. I was greeted by Toni at the front doors. A lady, Jeanette, walked over once I sat down. She introduced me to her husband and the pastor's wife. Apparently, the lead pastor started in late October, and the church is undergoing a number of changes.

I liked the sermon on Emmanuel—God with us in the past, present, and future. I was most impressed by how the service ended. The pastor shared a memory of his parents praying over him and his siblings on Christmas Eve. He then invited us to take communion and pray with our families. I came alone, so Jeanette came over and led me to the table. Her husband prayed that God would give me the desires of my heart, lead me, and guide me. We all had tears in our eyes when he finished. I plan to return, maybe when Mom and Dad are here.

December 22, 2015

So, I'm reading Revelation 9 when the fifth and sixth trumpet blasts unleash terror, torture, and death on all unbelievers (1/3 on earth will die). I should feel compassion and concern for their eternal well-being, but right now, I don't. God's wrath is just and holy. I am supposed to share my faith to win others to Christ, and yet I feel angry again. I'm angry at believers and nonbelievers for spending their lives doing things that do not matter. My role is not to judge them or push them away, but to love, serve, and forgive them.

I am living for something more. **I'm dying in my flesh and suffering in my mind for the call that God has given me.** It may not be evident to the outsider, but a tsunami has been ravaging my soul this year. It is all for my good and His glory.

January 3, 2016 [A New Beginning]

Happy New Year! My parents and I had the best visit ever! We had *so* much fun and got to experience many things: *The Nutcracker* in Fort Worth, Christmas lights on historic Main Street in Grapevine, the Gaylord Texan, Sunday worship at Abundant Life Church, IBC Christmas Eve service, and Buon Giorno Coffee, where Dad told of his travels across Europe in his Volkswagen camper. It was very memorable to have that quality time with my parents. I had their full attention, which makes me feel loved. Dad really enjoyed himself, and said so repeatedly.

Thursday was my last day at CGC. God has been faithful! I saw many 33s in December, especially during my last week at work. **My slogan is "33, He is with me!"** I feel peace and excitement as I enter this new season.

I'm at a coffee shop in Grapevine. Church was good. Guy and Jeanette came over to say hello before the service. I forgot to mention—on December 23 I received the ALC newsletter, a welcome call, *and* a written note from Pastor Jason. He said they are praying for me! It means a lot. I really like the church and the people seem so genuine and sincere. I signed up for the newcomer's class on January 10.

I've been writing for an hour—good practice for my future endeavors. Mom and Dad know that my project is to write about God's presence in my life.

I pray that 2016 is a year of answered prayers: friends, family, travel, and my book. A new church and new career enfold. It's all exciting!

God is so good!

PART III

THE AFTERMATH

CHAPTER 10

THE BLACK BOXES

A FLIGHT RECORDER, or "black box," is an electronic recording device used in aviation. It collects data that can be later accessed to identify and understand flight occurrences. My journals are like black boxes recording the mundane and significant events of my daily life. Not all of God's miracles and answered prayers were captured, and neither were all my trials and challenges. However, there is enough "data" to clearly show my evolution from living without God to accepting Christ, to walking with Jesus as a new believer, and then to flying with the Holy Spirit. The holy hijack was a success!

As you reviewed the "evidence" in PART II, I pray that you noticed:

1. I am weak and broken on my own. I am saved, sanctified, and *still* desperate for Jesus.

2. God is a rewarder of those who diligently seek Him. He answers prayers in various ways, in His perfect timing, according to His will.

3. Struggles, disappointments, trials, and unanswered prayers are all opportunities to draw closer to God through a personal relationship with Jesus.

4. The power of the Holy Spirit gives direction, comfort, wisdom, and peace. It also provides strength to lay down our desires, dreams, and needs so that we may willingly accept God's plan and purpose.

5. Prayer, surrender, and obedience are essential for spiritual transformation.

6. Journaling and sitting quietly in nature has brought me closer to Jesus.

I encourage you to get your own "black box" and begin recording the events of your life. If you capture your thoughts and feelings during a trial or difficult decision, you may find that you already have the answer. (That's God working in you via the Holy Spirit.) You just need to write it all out on paper—the good, the bad, and the ugly—and then sort through it. Pray as you write, silently in your head or write it out in the journal, and pray before you reread your entries.

Most importantly, look for patterns. Are you having the same conversation with the same person for the umpteenth time? Then that's a situation that needs consistent prayer and resolution. Are you stuck in a dead-end job? Then write about things you would like to do and pray for God to open doors. Are you suffering for obeying God's will? Then keep reading in the Bible, and I advise you to seek godly counseling and cultivate a strong prayer life.

The more you journal, the more you will glean when you look back at the entries. You will gain renewed clarity and be able to see the "invisible" fingerprints of God. Believe it or not, He *is* present in your daily life right now. Sometimes He's subtle, like a fluttering butterfly or a gentle breeze, and at other times He is more obvious, like a beautiful sunset or an answered prayer. "Draw near to God and He will draw near to you" (James 4:8 NKJV).

CHAPTER 11

THE TERRORIST

THE APOSTLE PAUL WAS a great man. He was transformed from a self-righteous persecutor of Christians to a humble servant of the Lord Jesus Christ who boldly proclaimed the Gospel at great personal cost. God opened his eyes to the truth, and he was transformed.

There is a well-known passage in the Bible (2 Corinthians 12) where Paul pleaded with the Lord 3 times to take away his thorn in the flesh. His thorn was something that caused him to sin or suffer repeatedly. God did not remove it because this affliction kept Paul humble and completely dependent on Him.

All followers of Jesus have a thorn. For years, I had no clue what mine was. Sure, I had numerous sinful behaviors, but which one was my thorn? As I matured in Christ, my list of habitual sin began shrinking. I began *choosing* new behaviors as I grew in awareness of God and the transforming power of the Holy Spirit. This resulted in new habits that glorified God. As a woman *still in the process* of becoming more like Jesus, I have finally identified the single sin that keeps me most dependent on God—anxiety.

Anxiety results from fearful responses to the mind's perception of possible dangers or outcomes. Distorted thoughts seem real, and the mind overprocesses to protect or prevent unfavorable situations. Based on my experiences, anxiety is a type of mental suffering. It pulls me to my knees and closer to my Savior.

My original coping strategy was to avoid situations that may trigger it. That helped to a degree, but resulted in my trying to control my environment or other people. I was only managing anxiety and still allowing fear to affect my life.

Now, when anxiety rises, I turn to God with a prayer for help and recite Scriptures out loud to counter the attack. I repeat them again and again until my mind calms down. Some call this "speaking truth over lies." Two of my favorites are: "For God has not given us a spirit of fear, but of power and of love, and of a sound mind" (2 Timothy 1:7 NKJV) and "You will keep in perfect peace all who trust in you, whose thoughts are fixed on you" (Isaiah 26:3 NLT).

Anxiety is a mental stronghold that the enemy uses to weaken us. Who is our enemy? The author of lies, prince of demons, and accuser of men; the rebellious angel cast out of heaven because he wanted to be equal with God. Satan opposes all good things. He seeks to control us by enslaving us to our sins. He plants seeds of fear, worry, and temptation in our minds every day, but most people are unaware of his subtle attacks.

Satan encourages *all of us* to sin. Whatever our flesh craves (selfish nature) is exactly what he provides. His purpose is to destroy God's most beloved creation—mankind (see John 10:10). Slowly and subtly he *binds* us in our sins to *blind* us from the truth of God's Word. Satan has controlled me through anxiety and fear—fear of rejection, fear of failure, and fear of not measuring up. My fears as a child prevented me from having my own voice and healthy boundaries.

Now that I'm a believer in Christ, I am called *daily* to put on the armor of God, to stand firm in all truth, and to continuously cast down every proud and lofty thing that exalts itself against the true knowledge of God (see 2 Corinthians 10:5). I stand against fearful thoughts, using the sword of the Spirit—the living Word of God (see Ephesians 6:17 and Hebrews 4:12). I speak it, read it, hear it, write it, sing it, and believe it as much as possible. This is how our minds are renewed over time.

In closing: "Don't copy the behavior and customs of this world, but let God transform you into a new person by changing the way you think. Then you will know what God wants you to do, and you will know how good and pleasing and perfect his will really is" (Romans 12:2 NLT).

CHAPTER 12

FLIGHT SAFETY CHECK

WHEN I ACCEPTED JESUS as my Savior, I received more than an emergency life jacket. He gave me a new flight plan (course of life), a new uniform (robe of righteousness), and a new title (child of the King). I received an operator's manual (Bible) and direct access to my Heavenly Father at any point in the journey (Holy Spirit). God watches over me from His control tower (heaven), and I reach Him via radio waves (prayer).

God knows my flight path at every moment and the location of all the other planes in the sky. Sometimes He routes me on a detour to avoid a dangerous storm. Other times He navigates me through heavy turbulence to test my structural integrity. There are many times when God directs me to keep circling because the runway is not cleared for landing. And rest assured, if the fuel gauge hits "E" and an engine dies, He knows exactly what to do.

There are no parachutes on board my Boeing 777, because God is my only life line. The Holy Spirit is my pilot, who took over when I surrendered to Christ. That leaves me as the copilot. I have enough rank to discuss my thoughts and suggestions, but ultimately the pilot is in control. He relays vital information from the control tower to instruct me. Problems arise if I alter the course (disobedience) or if the plane gets stuck at the gate (doubt and unbelief).

Many planes today are flying with only a copilot. The pilot was either left in the terminal or pushed out of the cockpit. These planes veer off course and cause collisions, because they do not have control tower access. They are trying to fly without God. Does this possibly describe your life? Is your plane going down as you frantically search for a parachute instead of allowing the pilot to take control? He is standing by, waiting to rescue you right now.

If you want to be saved, you must humbly and sincerely receive Jesus Christ as your Lord and Savior:

1. Believe Jesus is the Son of God who died on the cross to forgive your sins.
2. Believe Jesus rose from the dead to give you victory over sin and death.
3. Receive God's free gift of salvation and spend your eternity in heaven.

Flight safety check complete!

If you have completed the 3 steps above, then you are free to unfasten your seat belt and move about the cabin. Once you have regained your composure, please join the pilot in the cockpit, leaving all your personal baggage behind. Your new journey is about to begin!

Thank you for choosing Eternal Airlines. We hope you enjoyed your flight on this specially designed ALIVE aircraft. May we see you in the skies soon!

NOTES

PREFACE: LYRICS BY MERCYME

1. Composition/Song Title: THE HURT AND THE HEALER
   Writer Credits: Jim Bryson, Nathan Cochran, Bart Millard,
   Mike Scheuchzer, Robby Shaffer, and Barry Graul
   Copyright: © 2012 Simpleville Music/Wet As a Fish Music
   admin. by Fair Trade Music c/o Music Services. All rights
   reserved. Used by permission.

CHAPTER 9: INCREASING ALTITUDE AT IRVING BIBLE CHURCH

2. Paul David Tripp, *Instruments in the Redeemer's Hands*
   (Phillipsburg, N.J.: P&R Publishers, 2002), pp. 85-88.

BACK COVER: HIJACK DEFINITION

1. Webster's II New Riverside University Dictionary, s.v.
   "hijack."

2. This definition is the third of five for the word "hijack" in
   the Webster's II New Riverside University Dictionary. The
   number 3 has biblical and personal significance to the author.

ABOUT THE AUTHOR

CHARLOTTE BENKE grew up in Troy, Michigan, and earned a B.S.E. in Chemical Engineering from the University of Michigan in 1998. Her first career relocated her to Dallas, Texas, where she worked as a technical sales representative for a welding manufacturer. She received Jesus Christ as her Lord and Savior at the age of twenty-five, and it changed her life. Charlotte left sales in 2005 to pursue a Master's in the Art of Teaching at Texas Woman's University. After five years as a high school chemistry and physics teacher, she left teaching and stepped into the great unknown, praying that God would direct her to her next destination. After 3½ months of unemployment, Charlotte entered the financial services industry as an hourly contractor. By the end of 2015, she was laid off, much to her delight, because she felt called to write her testimony and transformation in Christ. God has led every step of her venture, opening doors and making connections. Charlotte believes that authoring this book is part of her divinely inspired purpose.
Join her journey at: www.alivehijackedbytheholyspirit.com.

www.ingramcontent.com/pod-product-compliance
Lightning Source LLC
Jackson TN
JSHW011947131224
75386JS00042B/1597